Gospel Hymns and Social Religion

The Rhetoric of Nineteenth-Century Revivalism

American Civilization

A Series Edited by Allen F. Davis

Gospel Hymns and Social Religion: The Rhetoric of Nineteenth-Century Revivalism
by Sandra S. Sizer (1978)

Social Darwinism: Science and Myth in Anglo-American Social Thought
by Robert C. Bannister (1979)

GOSPEL HYMNS AND SOCIAL RELIGION

The Rhetoric of Nineteenth-Century Revivalism

Sandra S. Sizer

Temple University Press
Philadelphia

Temple University Press, Philadelphia 19122

Published 1978
Printed in the United States of America

Library of Congress Cataloging in Publication Data

Sizer, Sandra S. 1946–
Gospel hymns and social religion.

(American civilization)
Based on the author's thesis, University of Chicago.
Includes bibliographical references and index.
1. Revivals—Hymns—History and criticism.
2. Revivals—United States. 3. Sociology, Christian—United States. I. Title. II. Series.
BV460.S58 264'.2 78-10165
ISBN 0-87722-142-1

To my first teachers,
John and Ruth Sizer

Contents

Preface

The studies which led to this book began during my graduate program at Miami University, where I first began serious study of American religions and first encountered anthropological theory, especially the work of Clifford Geertz and Claude Lévi-Strauss. These two areas, American religious history and comparative theory, provided the continuing impulse for my doctoral work in history of religions at the University of Chicago, where I completed the dissertation on which this book is based.

My dual interests have shaped the present study in various ways, particularly in my use of theories of language and culture, and of methods of analysis, which may be unfamiliar to some historians. I am convinced that it is important to be clear, within historical work itself, about theoretical perspectives and methods, and I have included discussions of such matters in the chapters which follow. I have tried to ensure that they would not intrude too much on the historical reconstruction of revivals and gospel-hymn rhetoric, which is the central purpose of the book, by confining the main body of theoretical discussion to the second half of Chapter 1, where I discuss the work of Geertz, Lévi-Strauss, and literary critic Kenneth Burke. From then on, the references to theoretical issues surface only occasionally; the reader is encouraged to consult the Notes and Appendix for further suggestions.

I am deeply grateful to those who worked with me

during my years at Miami University and the University of Chicago. Roland Delattre introduced me to the study of American religion and to the work of Geertz; later, Wayne Elzey sparked my interest in modern revivalism and in broader comparative theory, especially that of Lévi-Strauss. I wish also to thank Stan Lusby and Thomas Idinopulos for their encouragement and examples as teachers and scholars. At the University of Chicago, Charles Long urged me to pursue my interests in the Moody-Sankey era. Jonathan Smith, my adviser in history of religions, provided guidance throughout; whatever merit this study possesses in terms of theory and method is largely due to his incisive questions and suggestions. Jerald Brauer, my adviser in history of Christianity, continually encouraged me, by example and exhortation, to examine the history of revivalism from new perspectives. I am indebted to the insights of Donald Scott in the Department of History, who with Professors Smith and Brauer read and ably criticized the dissertation. A special thanks goes also to Joseph M. Kitagawa, who was helpful throughout my program.

Kenneth Arnold, Roland Delattre, and Peter Williams have read the manuscript and offered many helpful suggestions; I have also profited from the comments on Chapter 1 of Paula Fredriksen and John Gager. I want also to offer heartfelt thanks to the many others who have encouraged and taught me along the way—and first among these my parents, to whom this book is dedicated.

Abbreviations

The following abbreviations are used herein to refer to the five hymnals compared in Chapter 2:

GH Ira D. Sankey, James McGranahan, and George C. Stebbins, *Gospel Hymns Nos. 1 to 6 Complete* (1895; rpt. 1972).

H&M Thomas Hastings and Lowell Mason, *Spiritual Songs for Social Worship* (1832).

Lyre Joshua Leavitt, *The Christian Lyre* (1831; 26th ed., 1842).

Watts Isaac Watts, *Hymns and Spiritual Songs* (1707–9; rpt. 1819), Book II.

Wesley John Wesley, *A Collection of Hymns for the Use of the People Called Methodists* (1780; rpt., 1877).

Gospel Hymns and Social Religion

The Rhetoric of Nineteenth-Century Revivalism

1

The Gospel Hymns of Moody and Sankey: A Problem in Rhetorical Criticism

"IN England everybody is mad," the *New York Times* hypothesized in 1875, trying in vain to understand what the writer called "the Moody and Sankey fever" in the British Isles.[1] Dwight L. Moody and Ira D. Sankey were then just winding up an enormously successful two-year revival tour during which they had appeared before millions in England, Scotland, and Ireland; even Queen Victoria had remarked on the popularity of their meetings, although she declined invitations to attend. The two evangelists seemed to have hit upon what we would today call the right combination: Moody preached the gospel, and Sankey sang it.[2] They had thereby risen from the relative obscurity of Midwestern revival circuits to a modest international prominence, and over the next few years of American tours, mostly in Northern urban centers, they were to capture the country's imagination by their style.[3]

Moody and Sankey drew upon a long tradition of American revivalism, but they also made some significant contributions: their mass meetings in the largest auditoriums the cities had; their careful organization of "Christian workers" from local churches in each city; their completely interdenominational approach. They set the pattern for the tradition of urban revivalism that was to follow, the "crusade" structure (although that label came much later) associated most notably with Billy Sunday and Billy Graham. But perhaps the most remarkable feature of their work was Sankey himself. Besides being a powerful tenor, he was, by all accounts, a great favorite among the crowds and a charmer of the ladies. He had won over even the audiences in Scotland, long a bastion of conservatism with regard to hymn-singing and organ-playing (Sankey used the less obtrusive melodeon).[4] He was not the first singing evangelist; indeed Philip Phillips, the "Singing Pilgrim," had just preceded Moody and Sankey in the second of his own British campaigns.[5] Sankey, however, seemed to be able to draw his audiences into his performances in an irresistible way. Moreover, he had a way of perpetuating and enhancing his and Moody's images because he also had a popular product to sell: his books of songs.

When Sankey first arrived in Britain, he drew his material from Phillips's *Hallowed Songs,* one of many evangelical song collections then in general use in the United States. He also began, however, to add to his repertoire some arrangements of his own, and before long there arose a demand for their public circulation. When the publishers of *Hallowed Songs* refused to include his works as a supplement in the next edition, Sankey arranged with the firm of Morgan and Scott to bring out a folio of sixteen pages of his songs alone. That was the beginning of the British series, *Sacred Songs and Solos,* which in its numerous editions over the next several decades reportedly sold eighty million copies around the world.[6] When Sankey returned home in 1875, he found that P. P. Bliss and Major D. W. Whittle, another singing-preaching evangelistic team, had produced a hymn collection similar in style, called *Gospel Songs.* The two composers, Bliss and Sankey, agreed to combine their efforts and collaborate on a volume of revival songs, and *Gospel Hymns and Sacred Songs* appeared that same year.[7]

The popularity of the volume can, in one of Sankey's favorite phrases, better be imagined than described. Gospel meetings in Brooklyn and Philadelphia used it with, as Louis Benson put it, "a somewhat overwhelming effect," and it sold at least a million copies.[8] Encouraged by their success, the singers brought out a second number under the same title in 1876. Bliss died in December of that year in a train crash in Ashtabula, Ohio, but *Gospel Hymns,* as it was now titled, went on. Sankey enlisted the help of two other musical evangelicals, George C. Stebbins, who had worked with several preachers on the Midwestern circuits, and James McGranahan, who took Bliss's place as Whittle's assistant. The three men issued four more collections in the series over the next fifteen years, plus combined editions at the end of numbers four and six, the latter culminating in the marvelously titled "Diamond Edition" of 1894 and "Excelsior Edition" of 1895. Sales figures for the various editions remain unknown, but authorities agree that the series was by far the most successful of American hymnals. As music historian H. Wiley Hitchcock has observed, the final compilation "not only symbolizes the gospel-hymn movement of the late nineteenth century, but virtually embodies it between two covers."[9]

Clearly, a phenomenon of such immediate impact and long-range influence deserves some attention, some attempt to understand and account for it. One can, of course, point to Sankey's charm and Bliss's inopportune but heroic death (he could have saved himself from the train, said the newspaper accounts, but died trying to rescue his wife). There was also an important practical aspect with regard to selling the hymnals. It so happened that the two original compilers had access to two important music publishing houses, Bliss to the John Church Company in Cincinnati, which had published four volumes of his songs in the preceding four years, and Sankey to Biglow and Main in New York. John Church, organized in 1859, was by this time well established in general music publishing and had built a successful merchandising operation through local music retailers and a nationwide mail-order business. Biglow and Main was a younger firm, established in 1868 as a successor to William Bradbury's publishing house, which had sold his popular Sunday-school songbooks, but it had already become well known in the Sunday-school field and could service the New England area through its established outlets.[10] That combination gave Sankey immediate access to the media and, combined with Moody's increasing leadership over Northern evangelism, helped to make *Gospel Hymns* an outstanding success.

Yet those elements, while they help us understand the popularity of this particular collection of hymns, do not fully explain the appeal of the hymns themselves. If one asks the question, Why hymns at all? or, Why gospel hymns? the matter takes on additional dimensions of broader import in the study of American culture. The first number of *Gospel Hymns* was in many respects the culmination of a general movement in popular hymnody in the nineteenth century. In both music and lyrics it was similar to many other collections that had been appearing for two decades or more in response to the demand for simple, inexpensive hymnals for use in Sunday schools, Bible classes, and the like. The expansion of the Sunday-school movement in the 1830s and succeeding decades was followed by the "great prayer-meeting revival" of 1857–58, in whose wake the need for hymnals was greater than ever before. Concurrently, "services of praise" (that is, religious meetings devoted almost entirely to song) were being held in various parts of New England under the leadership of musician Eben Tourjée, and interest in music teachers' institutes was growing. Throughout New England and wherever that region's missionaries had traveled in the West, hymnals and songbooks sold in large numbers. To meet the demand, directors of choirs and music institutes had begun to produce collections of popular hymns.[11] William Bradbury, Asa Hull, George F. Root (who with his brother was associated with Root & Cady, a third important music publisher), William H. Doane, W. F. Sherwin, Robert Lowry—all those were well-known names in the field of Sunday-school music.[12] By adding perhaps half a dozen of their lesser-known associates and students plus the *Gospel Hymns* editors themselves, one can account for the authorship or arrangement of over seventy percent of the tunes (not, as we will see later, the lyrics) in the final collection of 739 hymns.[13] The men formed a school of sorts; for, either through teacher-student relationships or by association at musical conventions and institutes, they had often worked closely together. In addition, a few were linked backward to the work of Lowell Mason and Thomas Hastings, indisputably the leaders in teaching sacred music in the 1830s and 1840s.[14] *Gospel Hymns* was a direct descendant of that whole musical movement, and one cannot understand its appeal without taking into account this context.

Even more importantly, the development of a popular hymnody was closely connected with the nineteenth-century flowering of evangelicalism through the medium of revivals. That had been the case even in the eighteenth century, when many revival churches of the first Great Awakening had adopted Isaac Watts's *Psalms and Hymns* for their worship. In the nineteenth century, the frontier camp meetings of Kentucky and Tennessee, the upstate New York revivals led by Charles Grandison Finney, and the YMCA and Sunday-school movements closely associated with the 1857–58 revival had highlighted the use of hymns.[15] *Gospel Hymns* had roots stretching back several decades, into popular culture in general and into revivalism in particular.

The question, "Why gospel hymns?" is therefore connected to questions about the emergence of Moody-Sankey revivalism and to a host of other questions about popular religion in the white urban North, questions which should be of considerable interest to students of American culture and to historians of religions.[16] Yet very few have written on the subject of late nineteenth-century revivalism or hymnody, and fewer still have made any attempt to account for their development. William G. McLoughlin, Jr., whose book *Modern Revivalism: Charles Grandison Finney to Billy Graham* is the best work on the subject, links the Sankey hymns and Moody revivals to a general intellectual reorientation which took place, he says, between the Civil War and World War I.[17] But that finally begs the question. Why should there be such a reorientation? The usual answers range from generalizations about industrialization, urbanization, and socioeconomic mobility to allusions to the desire to hold onto the past ("old-time religion"). Such explanations are too general, not taking account of the particular content of revivalism, and they fail to face the problem of explaining the Moody-Sankey revivals in Britain, where conditions were not identical.

The subject of late nineteenth-century revivalism clearly deserves reconsideration. The popular hymnody of the period offers a base from which we can develop a different perspective on the matter, for the wide use and extensive sales of the hymns suggest that they can tell us a great deal about the world of those who wrote and sang them. Their lyrics ought to be representative of the religious language of the period, and a close analysis of them would afford us a point of entry into the world of revivalism. Of course, the hymns were set to music, and understanding the "language" of that music would undoubtedly help provide part of the explanation of hymns and revivals. Unfortunately, our current theories of musical meaning and our histories of American popular music are too sketchy to allow a nonmusicologist to draw conclusions about the relationship of the music to other cultural trends. Further, there is some justification for treating the lyrics separately. First, they had in part an independent existence, often appearing in religious periodicals as a poem without a tune. Second, during this period (roughly from 1850 to 1875) tunes began to derive their names from the words with which they were associated. Previously a tune had a separate name of its own; now, the *tune* was known as, say, "Bringing in the Sheaves" and was sung *only* with the words "Bringing in the Sheaves."[18] Third, singers and musicians themselves paid a great deal of attention to the words. Directions and models for singing emphasized the necessity of clear enunciation in order that the message would be adequately communicated.[19] Thus, while one hopes that students of the music will be able to enrich our understanding of the gospel-hymn movement, the lyrics of the hymns possess their own intrinsic interest as a central part of the language of revivalism.

To understand this language, to illuminate the meaning of the hymn lyrics, we will examine various aspects of revivalism and evangelicalism from the Finney period onward. In order to answer the question "Why gospel hymns?" it is important to consider what sorts of events and developments in American society made the hymns and the revivalist approach attractive to large numbers of people. I will not attempt to explain all of what McLoughlin calls the "reorientation" of American culture in the late nineteenth century, nor the British side of the revival phenomenon (although the approach would in theory be adaptable to that other context). The materials examined will, however, provide a context for understanding the gospel hymns in the setting of Moody-Sankey revivals and in the larger culture.

In short, I am proposing what might be called a "historical sociology of religious language." By this phrase I mean to suggest a perspective which employs insights and methods from several disciplines, especially those varieties of anthropology and literary criticism that emphasize cultural phenomena as linguistic phenomena intimately related to particular social settings. The approach is historical; it integrates interpretations of language and society into a narrative that shows continuities and changes in the phenomena described. The first element we must clarify is what the story is about, what it is a history *of*. Hence my emphasis on the use of language: I intend to show how a certain language developed in a particular tradition of American revivalism. Historians of American religion often have tended to neglect the specificity of linguistic forms; they have described what they take to be the essential content of beliefs, but paid little attention to the linguistic forms in which those beliefs are expressed, the ways they are used (for example, in ritual settings), and the specific situations of authors and audiences. There are of course exceptions to this generalization, notably in the history of colonial Puritanism since Perry Miller. But the task has yet to be done adequately for nineteenth-century popular religion. Here, sociology in the broad sense must go hand in hand with an intensive study of language if we are to make sense of the history of religion in America.

In this task, historians may fruitfully turn to other disciplines for ideas and methods. In anthropology, I have found most suggestive the different sorts of work done by Clifford Geertz and by Claude Lévi-Strauss. Geertz, who combines elements from the traditions of Max Weber and Emile Durkheim, is perhaps best known in the field of religious studies for his essay, "Religion as a Cultural System."[20] There he defines religion as a cultural symbol system which synthesizes, through ritual acts as cultural performances, both "ethos" (the socially patterned moods, motivations, attitudes—that is, a style of life) and "worldview" (belief system). This formulation is genuinely synthetic, but there are problems with it, especially with the elusive notion of "symbol." I find more promising his later interpretive essays, especially "Deep Play: Notes on the Balinese Cockfight" and "Thick Description: Toward an Interpretive Theory of Culture."[21] In these articles, he speaks of culture as an ensemble of "texts" to be interpreted, texts which themselves are embodiments of "complex conceptual structures" articulating culture as an "ideational" entity. The task of anthropologists is to immerse themselves in the societies they study and then to write a description (in his terms, "inscription") of those societies' ideas, expressive forms, all cultural activities as analogous to art. Each such form or activity is an interpretation of the society to itself, and the anthropologist attempts to "read over the shoulders" of the participants. One can see this perspective applied successfully in "Deep Play" and in the analysis of exemplary legends in *Islam Observed*—even though that book was written partly in the same vein as "Religion as a Cultural System."[22]

The emphasis on "texts," on cultural and religious activities as analogous to art forms, is an important move in interpretation, and it is one to which I shall turn in analyzing the gospel hymns. But there are areas left unclarified in Geertz's approach. Despite his own talents as an interpreter of culture, he does not elucidate as fully as he might the general theories or methods which underlie his own work. He has explicitly refused to develop broad comparative theory. For him, comparison functions only to set off two or more cultures in mutual relief and occasionally to provide a few wider concepts. Yet it is demonstrable that his work rests on certain kinds of theories.[23] Further, although his method relies on faithful translation, cross-culturally and historically, he provides few clues as to how we can perform such translation or judge its effectiveness. Interpretation seems dependent on intuition, with virtually no guidelines other than to immerse oneself in the "data." It is regrettable that Geertz has avoided developing broader theory, for his work thus encourages the lack of methodological self-consciousness already prevalent in historical studies. I believe, however, that his approach can be developed in fruitful directions if we take seriously his emphasis on "texts" and his espousal of the vocation of the literary critic. But we must be more explicit than he about the theories and methods of interpretation we use.

Particularly in the work of Claude Lévi-Strauss and his cousins in "cognitive anthropology" one can find helpful hints as to useful methods in analyzing "texts."[24] Working on models adapted from linguistics and deriving primary inspiration from Durkheim's work on classification, Lévi-Strauss and others have attempted to discern in texts the ideological structures, largely unconscious like rules of grammar, which form a lens or frame through which people see and acording to which they interpret the world. They are in accord with Geertz insofar as they hold that the "social construction of reality," in the phrase of sociologists Peter Berger and Thomas Luckmann,[25] involves a process of selection and integration by means of which a group constitutes its "world." But structuralists insist not only that the ideological frame must have a minimal coherence, as Geertz would agree, but further that the system follow logical rules of some sort. The most famous example stems from Lévi-Strauss's work on myths, where he claims that myths form a system of binary oppositions and mediations revolving around the dichotomy between "nature" and "culture."[26] The discovery of general principles of classification ultimately provides the basis for translation and interpretation.

Structural analysis is an extremely useful technique. Conscientiously employed, it generates fruitful hypotheses and new directions for investigation. Further, it genuinely reduces eisegesis (the pitfall of reading into a text anachronistic ideas or one's own notions of "what they must have meant"). Even looking for oppositions and mediations—which means paying attention to the use of specific words and metaphors, comparisons and contrasts, to identify what the author uses "to think with," in Lévi-Strauss's terms—is a good guideline to an interpretive procedure. It should not, however, become the end product. Attention to overall form, to genre, and to similar traditional concerns of the literary critic must play their part; and these in turn must be integrated with an understanding of the specific settings in which people produced the "texts" we are trying to read.[27]

In attempting to integrate these concerns, I have chosen to work from the concept of "rhetoric," as it has been most provocatively developed by literary critic Kenneth Burke.[28] Rhetoric is a useful concept in various ways. First of all, it calls to mind a situation of speech-making, of persuasion, which in turn suggests a slightly different perspective on the activity of the "social construction of reality": Changing the world necessitates changing the minds of those who construct reality, and that implies persuading them to accept a particular definition of it. The same necessity for persuasion holds if one is talking about preserving rather than changing the definition of the world; for it is not a question of inertia versus change but of the ongoing activity of maintaining a world of any sort. This perspective forces one to view each cultural phenomenon as part of a speaker (or writer) and audience relationship, with very definite social purposes. This of course does not deny an aesthetic dimension which might be understood as "expressive," wherein an artist, or a preacher or a hymnist, is trying to articulate deep feelings through a given form. Nor does it ignore the "logical" dimension, the aim of creating a coherent, orderly (and therefore more convincing) world picture; in that respect the structuralists have made great advances in seeking out implicit systems of order. But focusing on the *rhetorical* aspect can provide, first, a much-needed emphasis on usage of language and, through that, a more adequate approach to the problem of the relation between text and social situation.[29]

Burke highlights that relation by defining rhetoric as a "strategy for encompassing a situation."[30] Cultural forms understood as "strategies" would thus be problem-solving tools (as structuralism also insists) operating within certain rule-bounded contexts. The contexts include rules of grammar, selection of appropriate vocabulary ("diction," as classical rhetorical criticism would have it), and literary form. Disclosing the strategy of a work requires attention to the author's choice of language, modes of structuring his discourse, and the forms chosen for his "text." Particularly, one must consider the question of what is communicated by certain *types* of structures. All the peculiar conventions of grammar, vocabulary, and style are part of rhetorical strategy which are open to analysis by the critic.[31]

The term "strategy" implies that conscious intention is operative in the author's choice of language; yet authors and speakers are not always fully conscious of the techniques they use and why they are effective. As Burke himself has admitted, the word is perhaps too strong in that respect.[32] Certainly there are many levels of unconscious structure, beginning with grammar, which the users of a language may not be able to explicate. Nevertheless one can reasonably say that, given the familiar and unsystematized structures and forms available to members of a social group, people learn to manipulate them in particular ways for particular effects, even if they learn only by trial and error, and even if some never learn to become as effective as others. A political candidate who makes an unfortunate ethnic slur learns quickly to pay closer attention to his choice of metaphors or he will lose the election. A woman whose novel sells a million copies can recognize her success, as can others who may try to "cash in" on her "formula," although neither she nor they might be able to give a satisfactory explanation of the book's popularity. In this way we can speak of strategies "learned" as one learns the proper use of grammar, by imitation and by being corrected (or misunderstood, or ignored). Rather than insist that such strategies must be either explicit and conscious or hidden inside people's heads in a mysterious realm of "rules," we can look for traditional models available to authors, models which they may have chosen to imitate. Such models could become paradigms whose implicit "rules" or "strategies" become the governing principles for a whole class of imitations. This describes precisely what happened in the tradition of popular hymnody in the nineteenth century, but discussion of that must be reserved for Chapter 5.

Further, the notion of strategy must be broadened to include many levels of problem-solving. The purpose of some texts is to generate a response to a very specific event—for example, an Election Day sermon in the Puritan context. Others may deal with more general problems which nevertheless have definable boundaries, like a temperance tract with lessons that can be applied to a variety of situations having in common only that someone is consuming an alcoholic beverage. Still others have a much broader range, like texts embodying the cosmological speculations of Indian philosophers or the theodicies of Christian apologists. These seem more distant from specific problems. Yet because of their broader range and greater distance, texts of the latter sort can become models, not only because they are imitated but also because they provide a comprehensive interpretive framework under which one can subsume other problems. Further, some texts, especially those deriving from ritual performances, provide a technique for participation, as does a meditation manual. The gospel hymns are most obviously an example of the last type of text, because they encourage participation by singing; but they also represent a general description of the world. They do not offer an abstract philosophical system, yet they do operate at a distance from everyday activities and social issues. As such they represent strategies for solving general problems about the relations of human beings to each other and to the spiritual forces or beings of their universe.

The extension of the term "strategy" to unconscious as well as conscious operations and to many kinds of texts stretches the term rather far. I use it nevertheless, in order to highlight the relationship between text and social situation and to keep in the forefront the question of the intention of the authors in any given case—how they perceived their situation, their allies and opponents, the problems which they thought needed to be solved. I prefer "strategy" to a term like "expression," which allows the interpreter to slip too easily into treating the text as purely aesthetic or purely religious, without considering the social world of which it is a part—the "situation," in Burke's terminology. In this connection, Burke introduces a notion which will be especially useful in considering the context of the hymns: the concept of "identification." This term captures another aspect of rhetorical criticism. Since the situation which rhetoric seeks to encompass is a situation of persuasion, therefore of debate and argument, we cannot view its definitions of the world merely as abstract systems. Rather, we must see them as strategic definitions proposed over against other definitions offered by opponents. The rhetor's world is not that of the solipsist; it is one of conflicting claims and avid argumentation. In adopting a particular strategy, one attempts to stake out a territory and persuade others to join. Thus rhetoric involves that aspect of the human condition whereby people express and recognize their mutual affinities, their belonging to the same group, and especially, to *this* group and not *that.* Rhetoric recognizes the divisions among people into various classes of beings;[33] rhetorical criticism seeks to make clear what the "identifications" are, and how the "belonging" is conceived.[34]

In considering the gospel hymns, community identification is crucial in understanding their significance. We must pay close attention to questions of the authorship of materials, to the positions of authors and audiences in society, and to similar factors familiar from the sociology of knowledge. Yet in some cases (including the one at hand) we may not be able to deduce immediately the nature of the "debate" which we presume to be going on. If we read the speeches of New England Congregationalist ministers in the early 1800s, for example, we might imagine that the country stood in imminent danger of being taken over by an army of atheistic Frenchmen, and that they were the opponents. But in fact the enemy was largely an invented one. Ministers were employing the image of the "infidel" for its strategic value, to bring a political question into the moral realm, where they could exert greater influence. In yet more subtle instances, new strategies spring up but with no opponents identified. One can easily identify the "Old Lights" and "New Lights" who, in the aftermath of the Great Awakening of the eighteenth century, argued over the propriety and utility of revivals. But it would be a more difficult enterprise to try to explain the earliest revivals as directed against some opponent. Were the members of Jonathan Edwards's Northampton congregation defining themselves over against another group by becoming a "revival church"? And how could we answer such a question, if we find no direct evidence of "debate"? That sort of problem arises frequently in attempting to discuss religious expressions as rhetoric, because religious spokesmen often pretend that they offer the only conceivable alternative, that they are pronouncing pure doctrine or the undefiled message of the Bible, as though no possible argument existed—and understandably enough, since their claims are absolute. But that would mean, as Burke also suggests, that "identifications" can be disguised or only partially articulated, like the principles of rhetorical strategy. Nevertheless, we can often discover them through careful investigation.

In light of the concept of rhetoric, I propose to show how, in the gospel hymns, form and metaphor articulate a structure of the world and simultaneously create a community with its own specific identity. The hymns represent an interpretive strategy and a technique of transcendence. "Transcendence" can be understood soteriologically: the hymns serve as a vehicle of religious experience, uplifting the soul and bringing it nearer to God. I wish to understand the term sociologically: the hymns create a sacred community, raising the group and its members above the lesser beings which inhabit the world. To understand how such transcendence comes about, we must above all pay close attention to the particular strategies and rhetorical techniques employed by the authors of the hymn lyrics.

For that reason the chapters which follow are devoted largely to an analysis of strategy, the language of the hymns and of the world of meaning in which they participate. Examining this language historically, I will be moving back and forth between the 1870s and the 1820s. I do not, however, intend this study to be a thoroughgoing history of revivalism during the intervening years. My primary task is to interpret the kind of hymn found in the *Gospel Hymns* collection. To that end I have made use of sources from other periods and situations, but I have been highly selective, attempting not to cover all the ground that might conceivably be relevant but rather to choose representative sources which mark significant developments connected with important features of gospel-hymn rhetoric. What those features were, we will see in Chapter 2.

2

Passivity and Passion: The Strategy of the Gospel Hymns

MOODY and Sankey found themselves not only salesmen of salvation, as some have described them, but also indirectly salesmen of books of gospel hymns. By looking carefully at these hymns we can begin to develop a deeper understanding of the strand of American religion which they represent. We must begin with a close analysis of what these hymns are, what kind of "text," in Geertz's terms, we have before us. Sankey's final compilation, *Gospel Hymns Nos. 1 to 6,* will be the central focus; yet it is curious first of all because it does not include only gospel hymns. The compilers tell us that the Excelsior Edition includes besides the gospel hymns "over 125 of the most useful and popular STANDARD HYMNS AND TUNES OF THE CHURCH."[1] I chose this collection because of its representativeness and its large number of hymns; but as it stands it does not quite suit our purposes. One of the things we wish to discover is the distinctive features which gospel hymns possessed, as contrasted with other kinds of hymns. Thus if we examined this book in its entirety as a supposedly uniform collection, we might be led astray in our search. The compilers clearly intended the gospel hymns to be the primary focus, but their apparent desire to make the book a complete edition of popular songs—and perhaps to appeal to churchly circles as well as revival audiences—led them to include other kinds of hymns. The hymnal includes psalm arrangements inherited from the Puritan tradition, and some of Isaac Watts's and Charles Wesley's hymns from the eighteenth century; and it even opens with a sixteenth-century lyric, William Kethe's "All people that on earth do dwell" set to the familiar "Old Hundred" tune.[2] Those should not be included in an analysis that seeks to explain the primary appeal of the gospel hymn. Thus we must first stipulate what hymns from the collection are to be regarded as belonging to this category.

It is impossible to define the term "gospel hymn" from some intuitive notion of its form or content, since that is what we eventually wish to derive. But unfortunately, there are few other clues that can aid us. The arrangement of hymns within the book provides no answer. It reflects no liturgical or seasonal scheme, as one might find in high-church hymnals; there is no plan of rotation, such as the New England Puritans followed in singing their metrical psalms. One might expect a topical arrangement, such as Watts intended for his *Psalms and Hymns* of the early eighteenth century, or the different sort of scheme used in John Wesley's *A Collection of Hymns for the Use of the People Called Methodists* (1780), where hymns were arranged according to areas of the individual Christian's spiritual life.[3] The latter seems to be the way in which the British counterpart of Sankey's hymnal, *Sacred Songs and Solos,* was arranged. But the American version was different. It contains a topical index to general themes which might be employed to correlate hymns with sermon or meeting topics, but the hymns themselves follow no discernible principle of order. The few "special occasion" hymns (for example, for Sabbath, communion, evening worship, farewell) are scattered randomly, and the pre-nineteenth-century psalms and hymns are mixed in with more recent compositions, although their concentration is greater in the last quarter of the book. The compilers seem to have arranged the hymnal so that one could pick almost any of the hymns and expect to find "the gospel" there.

Another approach to the question is to inquire about the manner in which Sankey and his associates compiled the book—where they obtained the hymn lyrics and whether there were representative groups of authors whose hymns are the best sources. Such questions do not take us far; for, unlike the tunes which, as noted in Chapter 1, were for the most part composed by musicians from an identifiable "school," the hymn lyrics seem to have come from nowhere in particular. There are a few recurring names, of course. Some composers, notably P. P. Bliss and Robert Lowry, wrote their own lyrics, but many—including Sankey, McGranahan, and Stebbins—did not. Some requested others to write hymns for their tunes, sometimes even engaging the services of a professional. George F. Root and later William Bradbury, for example, contracted with the famous blind hymnist Fanny Crosby to supply a certain number of hymns; they were most fortunate, since Crosby was extremely prolific (she is said to have written eight thousand hymns).[4] Most often, however, songbook compilers drew on other songbooks or on devotional poems published in religious periodicals.[5] International copyright laws did not exist, so British material could be pirated; and while newspapers were theoretically subject to copyright laws, these laws were rarely invoked.[6] Thus hymnbook compilers had access to a wide range of virtually anonymous material. As a result, we know little about most authors of such lyrics other than their names, and we have no record of why certain kinds of lyrics were preferred to others.

This situation requires that we stipulate the boundaries for the term "gospel hymn" in some other way than by internal structure or research into sources. I have chosen to include only those hymns written after 1820, for several reasons. From the viewpoint of *Gospel Hymns* and its lyric sources, the first two decades of the nineteenth century represent a dry spell in hymnwriting; but after 1820 the number of hymns included increases in each decade, with the great surge beginning around 1850. Only after 1820 are American hymnists in the majority, the earlier hymns being predominantly British. A similar shift occurs in the relative proportions of male and female authors: although men (primarily clergy) still dominated the field, women's contributions increased significantly, amounting to nearly one-third of the post-1820 hymns in the collection. We will be able to understand the significance of this sociological difference later (see Chapter 4).[7] Since the undated hymns are more likely to be of later composition than earlier,[8] we can include 615 of the 739 hymns in Sankey's collection as likely to be representative of the gospel hymn "type." That still leaves a body of hymns with a considerable range of composition dates (seventy years) and a somewhat heterogeneous group of authors (American and British, male and female, perhaps rural and urban). But they are homogeneous in that most authors were Protestant evangelicals, especially Methodists and Baptists. More surprisingly, they were, with only one exception, Northerners. This will be significant in light of the argument I will develop in Chapter 6. For now, the definition of the gospel hymn "text" as those lyrics in *Gospel Hymns Nos. 1 to 6* written after 1820 provides us with a narrower group within justifiable boundaries. It is a happy coincidence that we have eliminated 124 hymns, almost the same number as the compilers suggested were not gospel hymns but standard church hymns.

The next step after establishing the basic text is to specify methods for analyzing its various features to determine what is distinctive about the rhetoric of the gospel hymn. (The full explication and justification for these methods appears in the Appendix; here I will only describe briefly their principal features.) I have chosen three dimensions for analyzing the rhetoric: metaphor, theme, and form. With regard to the first: it is clear from even a superficial reading that the gospel hymns are largely constructed around series of metaphors in poetic form—Jesus as "shepherd"; life as a "stormy sea"; the individual as a "child" of God. Structural analysis shows that such metaphors consistently appear as elements in a group of contrasting sets. The hymns are sharply dualistic in this respect, describing the world and its woes in opposition to the bliss of heaven and the beauty of Jesus. Some typical sets of contrasts appear clearly in the following hymn by Frances Havergal, the famous British counterpart to America's Fanny Crosby:

Light after darkness, Gain after loss,
  Strength after weakness, Crown after cross;
  Sweet after bitter, Hope after fears,
  Home after wandering, Praise after tears.

Sheaves after sowing, Sun after rain,
  Sight after mystery, Peace after pain,
  Joy after sorrow, Calm after blast;
  Rest after weariness, Sweet rest at last.

Near after distant, Gleam after gloom,
  Love after loneliness, Life after tomb,
  Bliss after agony, Raptures of bliss,
  Right was the pathway Leading to this.

(GH 193)[9]

Although the structure of that hymn is unusually monotonous, the before-and-after pattern clearly exhibits an important feature of the gospel hymns: sets of polar values like light/darkness, strength/weakness, sweetness/bitterness, hope/fear, home/wandering, and so on. And some of these expressions obviously represent the same kinds of contrasts: "joy after sorrow" is only a different way of expressing "bliss after agony." When the whole system is elucidated, it becomes clear that certain classes of metaphors belong together (see the Appendix). Generally, dualism between "the world" and heaven or Jesus is articulated primarily by means of seven sets of contrasts: (1) negative versus positive emotions, as in joy/sorrow, love/fear; (2) turmoil versus rest, as in a stormy sea versus a safe harbor, or wandering in the wilderness versus arriving home; (3) weakness versus strength, as in the sick being healed or burdens being lifted; (4) darkness versus light, as in night/day, shadows/sunshine; (5) battle versus victory; (6) purity versus impurity, as when the sinner is "washed white as snow"; and (7) guilt versus atonement, as when the debtor's debt is paid by Jesus, the rebel is forgiven. Such sets of contrasts are important rhetorical devices in all the hymns, but they vary in their frequency of use and emphasis. Variations are especially significant when compared to other kinds of hymns. My description of the distinctive features of the gospel hymn, in terms of its "content," rests primarily on an analysis of the metaphors.

Nevertheless, we should also examine another aspect of content primarily as a means of cross-checking the "micro" analysis of metaphors, namely that of theme. Theme is understood simply as the answer to the question, "What is this hymn about?" The answers might be, "Christ's sacrifice," "God's kingship," "the beauty of Jesus," "the glories of heaven," or "the pilgrimage of the Christian." There are multiple possibilities, but most of them are directly related to the kinds of portrayals of the world found in the sets of metaphors. A few important kinds of hymns—notably those of battle, heaven, pilgrimage, and mission—appear more prominent here than in the microscopic analysis of language in terms of metaphors.

The third dimension of analysis is the form of the hymns. Not only what the hymns say, but how they say it, reveals something about the way the relations among human beings or between humans and deities are conceived. I wish to call particular attention to one very important aspect of form, namely the hymns' mode of address. Some hymns call upon the deity in praise or prayer; others are addressed to a specific audience, either sinners or Christians, still others have no clearly defined audience but seem to be simple descriptions or affirmations. Those differences mark the most important formal distinctions among hymns within the gospel-hymn type, and in comparison with other sorts of hymns.

My arguments for the distinctive character of the rhetoric are based on a comparison of gospel hymns with samples from four earlier hymnals. The first is Isaac Watts's *Hymns and Spiritual Songs* (1707–9), a classic of Protestant hymnody written under the influence of the British tradition of psalmody; I have drawn my material from Book II, which comprises Watts's own "free composures."[10] John Wesley's *Collection* of 1780, many of the hymns in which were written by his brother Charles, is another British classic, originally designed as a supplement to the regular liturgy of the Anglican church.[11] The two other hymnals are revival songbooks from the Finney era: Joshua Leavitt's *The Christian Lyre* (1831) represents the West, and Thomas Hastings and Lowell Mason's *Spiritual Songs for Social Worship* (1832) the East, in that tradition. In Chapter 3 we will see more specifically the significance of each. As it turns out, the four other hymnals represent a kind of continuum, with Watts's being furthest away from *Gospel Hymns* in terms of form and content, while Leavitt's collection is closest. In the interpretation which follows we will see the nature of the similarities and differences.

If we were to simulate a debate between Watts and Sankey on the nature of the human condition, the question might well be put as "Human Beings: Worms or Wanderers?" Watts's strategy is to portray human beings as low, vile, unworthy creatures, to convict them of sin and guilt and then to persuade them of the need for atonement. The emphasis on guilt and atonement is important in the three succeeding hymnals as well. Its classic expression appears in Watts's famous verse:

Alas! and did my Saviour bleed!
And did my Sov'reign die?
Would he devote that sacred head
For such a worm as I?
(Watts 9.1)

The "worm" is all the more despicable because he tries to exert his will against God, the ruler of all; that is, he is a *rebel* worm, a blasphemer, a criminal, a backslider, an upstart challenging God's rightful government; and such a worm deserves only to be damned.[12] Indeed, the rebel is accused of the most heinous crimes of the universe:

Hearts of stone, relent, relent,
Break by Jesus' cross subdu'd;
See his body, mangled, rent,
Cover'd with a gore of blood:
Sinful soul, what hast thou done?
Crucified th' incarnate Son!
(H&M 35.1)

The only solution to the problem is first the mediation of Jesus, and second the submission of the rebel. Jesus's death is the mediating act, understood as the sacrifice on behalf of human beings, the "ransom" which "paid the debt." In addition, hymns like these often portray Jesus as an advocate for human beings before God's throne, where the sinner can only utter a plea for undeserved mercy:

> Prostrate, dear Jesus, at thy feet
> A guilty rebel lies;
> And upward to the mercy-seat
> Presumes to lift his eyes.
>
> O, let not justice frown me hence;
> Stay, stay the vengeful storm;
> Forbid it, that Omnipotence
> Should crush a feeble worm.
>
> (H&M 3.1–2)

Omnipotence, fortunately, has no desire to step on worms; the result is "pardon," "redemption," "mercy."

That kind of language is by no means foreign to the gospel hymns, but its presence is much reduced. Moreover, the emphasis has shifted in the contexts in which such language occurs. Although there are many references to the guilt of the sinner, the stronger language—rebel, criminal, blasphemer—has almost disappeared. On the other hand, terminology of redemption and reconciliation, the positive side of this class of metaphors, is very common, suggesting an accent on salvation more than on sin. A good example is P. P. Bliss's "Once for All":

> Free from the law, oh, happy condition,
> Jesus hath bled, and *there* is remission,
> Curs'd by the law and bruised by the fall,
> Grace hath redeemed us once for all.
>
> (GH 13.1)

The legal elements are all present, yet the former scenario of a court of judgment is softer and more diffuse. In Bliss's portrayal, it is not that people willfully disobeyed the law or sinned of their own accord, but rather they were "curs'd *by* the law," "bruised *by* the fall," as if they were not active agents in the matter at all.

This intriguing twist in the legal language turns out to be in accord with the dominant tone of *Gospel Hymns,* where human beings are essentially victims of evil, impersonal forces. They are not worms but wanderers—exiles or pilgrims, accidentally cast out on foreign shores—as in Sankey's famous solo, "Where Is My Wandering Boy Tonight?" (GH 631).[13] This theme appears again and again: the human fate is to roam aimlessly under the scorching desert sun through vast stretches of wilderness or to be tossed mercilessly on stormy seas. Burdens, toil, struggle, and strife are the common lot, as in J. B. Matthias's vivid portrayal, "Deliverance Will Come":

I saw a wayworn trav'ler in tatter'd garments clad,
  And struggling up the mountain, it seemed that he was sad;
  His back was laden heavy, his strength was almost gone,
  Yet he shouted as he journeyed, Deliverance will come.

The summer sun was shining, the sweat was on his brow,
  His garments worn and dusty, his step seemed very slow:
  But he kept pressing onward, for he was wending home;
  Still shouting as he journeyed, Deliverance will come.
(GH 225.1–2)

That hymn has an optimistic tone, for it is about a Christian, still a wanderer, but assured of a happy ending to the journey. Similar images, however, apply to the sinner:

Oh, soul toss'd on the billows,
  Afar from friendly land,

Look up to Him who holds thee
In "The hollow of His hand."
(GH 270.1)

The appeal of images of storm, desert, wandering and the like is extremely strong. We must, however, avoid the temptation to interpret them too literally. Shipwreck themes do not "symbolize" the fact that late nineteenth-century Americans were fascinated with wrecks at sea (although they were); nor does the pilgrim motif refer to a collective memory of the frontier or to socioeconomic mobility and rootlessness, important as those may turn out to be at another level. We must understand such images first of all in the context of the internal language system of the hymns and the hymnodic tradition, that is, at the level of rhetoric as such. Within that system, the import of images of turmoil and restless movement is their representation of the individual no longer as willfully evil, as the rebel worm, but as the passive recipient of blows dealt by inimical impersonal forces.

This is indeed the first important strategic move of gospel-hymn rhetoric: to portray the human condition as that of a passive victim. The solution to the difficulty is equally passive: to rest in some safe place. Those who are saved hide "in the hollow of God's hand," in the bosom of Jesus, or in the cleft of the Rock of Ages; they find safety in a lifeboat which lands at a quiet shore or harbor; the journey ends at "home." We find this, for example, in an unusual hymn—unusual in that it is written in Scottish dialect—of the period:

Like a bairn to its mither, a wee birdie to its nest,
I wad fain be ganging noo unto my Saviour's breast,
For he gathers in his bosom witless, worthless lambs like me,
An' he carries them himsel', to his ain countrie.
(GH 417.3)

Metaphors of hiding, safety, and refuge are especially prominent in the gospel hymns and in Leavitt's *The Christian Lyre*. Yet earlier hymns often focused on the theme of Jesus as refuge or haven from the storm. The distinctive feature here is not only that the authors of the gospel hymns used such language more extensively, but that they also developed a genre of hymns which described the final, ultimate refuge—namely, hymns of heaven. *Gospel Hymns* includes ninety-six such hymns, including those which speak of heaven as the "Last Day"—premillennial hymns. This is an enormous proportion of hymns to be devoted to one topic, and it represents a sharp increase over the numbers devoted to descriptions of heaven in the other hymnals, even the *Lyre*. Heaven is essentially a home, a haven, a place of rest, a "happy shore," as in the familiar "Sweet By and By":

> There's a land that is fairer than day,
> And by faith we can see it afar;
> For the Father waits over the way,
> To prepare us a dwelling-place there.
>
> In the sweet by and by,
> We shall meet on that beautiful shore,
> In the sweet by and by,
> We shall meet on that beautiful shore.
> (GH 204.1, Ch)

Heaven and the afterlife thus come into prominence as a complement to Jesus as the Rock of Ages: rest and safety become the promise of a future life as well as being a feature of an immediate relationship with the deity.

It is appropriate to observe at this point an interesting feature of many of the heaven hymns, one which they share with many pilgrim hymns. Often they emphasize the transient nature of this-worldly life by using verbs in their progressive forms, thus making grammar conform to the content they express. Scottish clergyman Horatius Bonar's "Beyond the Smiling and the Weeping" makes extensive use of the device:

> Beyond the smiling and the weeping,
> I shall be soon, I shall be soon,
> Beyond the waking and the sleeping,
> Beyond the sowing and the reaping,
> I shall be soon, I shall be soon.
>
> Beyond the parting and the meeting,
> I shall be soon, I shall be soon.
> Beyond the farewell and the greeting,
> Beyond the pulse's fever beating,
> I shall be soon, I shall be soon.
>
> (GH 602.1–3)

The contrast between the "-ing" forms and the measured, evenly accented "I shall be soon" serves to reinforce the contrast between the changing world below and the unchanging one above. In this hymn, incidentally, the effect is musical as well, as Stebbins wrote the "beyond" phrases in quarter and eighth notes and the "I shall be soon" phrases in half and quarter notes. That produces an effect of change in tempo from one "world" to another, from slow to fast, dynamic to static, "turmoil" to "rest." As the above example shows, too, the hymns of heaven are no more active than others; salvation is accomplished by simple translation ("I will be there") or, at most, by the action of Jesus ("He'll carry me over Jordan").[14]

Even the portrait of Jesus does not reveal much in the way of vigorous activity, however. Except on the rare occasions when he is rushing to help his beleaguered army—or promising to rush there, anyway—his activity is mostly limited to carrying people across the river or walking with them, guiding them down a path. Jesus invites people to come to him; he "stands at the door and knocks"; but he is no longer the active king-conqueror or the lawyer-advocate of Watts. In Watts, it is not at all unusual to find a description of the majestic creator:

Long ere the lofty skies were spread,
Jehovah fill'd his throne;
Or Adam form'd, or angels made,
The Maker liv'd alone.

His boundless years can ne'er decrease,
But still maintain their prime;
Eternity's his dwelling-place,
And *ever* is his time.
(Watts 17.1)

In the gospel hymns, the character has changed:

What a friend we have in Jesus,
All our sins and griefs to bear!
What a privilege to carry
Everything to God in prayer!
(GH 583.1)

Jesus is the focus, not as the distant creator deity but as a friend; nor does he rush out to do battle with the chaotic forces that are overpowering humankind. The secret of his saving power lies in a movement inward, not only toward shelter and refuge with Jesus and/or in heaven, but to a realm of intimacy. It is a sphere not only of passivity but of passion—the passions, the emotions, in nineteenth-century language the "affections." In that realm the individual by relying on Jesus achieves inward control to counter the turbulent world and his own evil passions; strength is generated internally by gaining control of emotions, turning them into positive forces by focusing them on Jesus alone. This is the second preeminent strategy of gospel-hymn rhetoric.

In some respects, this strategy too has its precursors in the language of some of the other hymnals, where songs often define the individual in terms of emotional categories. The sinner is full of "sorrow" and "woe," is "grieved," "despairing," "fearful," as in this verse:

> Master, with anguish of spirit
> I bow in my grief to-day;
> The depths of my sad heart are troubled,
> Oh, waken and save, I pray!
> Torrents of sin and of anguish
> Sweep o'er my sinking soul;
> And I perish! I perish, dear Master;
> Oh! hasten, and take control.
>
> (GH 261.2)

That kind of formulation might be found in any of the hymnals with the possible exception of Watts, although it should be observed that "torrents" of sin and anguish "sweeping over" the soul carry the distinctively late nineteenth-century connotation of being oppressed by uncontrollable forces—now clearly *within* the person. Aside from that, however, it is a familiar strategy to define the problem as deriving from the realm of the emotions. And, if the sin-sickness is emotional, so is the cure. Fanny Crosby's well-known lyric, "Rescue the Perishing," is unlike those of earlier hymnals because it is a missionary hymn of a certain style (to be discussed below) but its emphasis on the inward restoration of the emotions is otherwise typical:

> Down in the human heart,
> Crush'd by the tempter,

Feelings lie buried that grace can restore:
  Touched by a loving heart,
  Wakened by kindness,
Chords that were broken will vibrate once more.
(GH 592.3)

The heart is the seat of the problem, and the relationship with Jesus is a matter of the heart.

Further, as one would expect, all the hymnals portray Jesus as a deity of love: "gentle," "tender," "sweet," "a Friend."

Hear the sweet voice of Jesus,
  Full, full of love;
 Calling tenderly, calling lovingly,
  "Come, O sinner, come."
(GH 122.Ch)

But the gospel hymns elaborate this point much further. The love of Jesus is by no means a general or abstract love, or one of mere pity or compassion. Pity, mercy, and compassion often appear in earlier hymnals as equivalent to love, carrying a slight connotation of a hierarchical relationship, of a great and magnanimous figure looking down on benighted humankind out of some mysterious love. Such connotations have almost entirely disappeared from the gospel hymns. The relationship has become much more intimate: although Jesus may be stronger, he is not higher. The hymns tell us that Jesus is not only loving and kind, but also charming and beautiful; he enfolds the poor sinner in his arms, and to be in his presence is heavenly bliss. "I am thine, and Thou art mine," they often proclaim.

The hymns reveal numerous variations on the theme of intimacy, devotion, and an emotional relationship. Some are written from the point of view of an admirer, focusing on the beauty of Jesus's person. One of the best examples, which interestingly borrows its imagery from the Song of Songs, is from the *Lyre:*

This is my Beloved, his form is divine,
His vestments shed odors around,
The locks on his head are as grapes on the vine,
When autumn with plenty is crown'd.

His voice as the sound of the dulcimer sweet,
Is heard through the shadow of death,
The cedars of Lebanon bow at his feet,
The air is perfumed with his breath.

His lips as a fountain of righteousness flow,
To water the gardens of grace;
From which their salvation the Gentiles shall know
And bask in the smiles of his face.

(Lyre 55.5–7)

Other hymns place a special accent on the human being's dependence on Jesus for strength, consolation, and companionship. Familiar lyrics like "I Need Thee Every Hour" (GH 597) and "What a Friend We Have in Jesus" (GH 583) are good examples. The following hymn, "In the Secret of His Presence," while not well known today, was held up as exemplary by Sankey because its author, Ellen Lakshmi Goreh, was a high-caste Indian woman converted by Christian missionaries. It captures the atmosphere of sweet communion with Jesus as a special confidant and source of strength and refreshment:

In the secret of His presence how my soul delights to hide!
Oh how precious are the lessons which I learn at Jesus' side!
Earthly cares can never vex me, neither trials lay me low;

For when Satan comes to tempt me, to the secret place I go,
To the secret place I go.

When my soul is faint and thirsty, 'neath the shadow of His wing
There is cool and pleasant shelter, and a fresh and crystal spring;
And my Saviour rests beside me, as we hold communion sweet:
If I tried I could not utter what He says when thus we meet,
What He says when thus we meet.

Only this I know: I tell Him all my doubts, my griefs and fears;
Oh how patiently He listens! And my drooping soul He cheers:
Do you think he ne'er reproves me? What a false friend He would be,
If He never, never told me of the sins which He must see,
Of the sins which He must see.

(GH 363.1–3)

That hymn is an early expression of precisely the kind of romantic lyric about Jesus of which the later "In the Garden" ("I come to the garden alone") is now the paradigm.

In all these hymns, the intimate relationship with Jesus itself brings salvation. Entering into this intimate sphere the devotee finds that negative emotions are transformed into positive ones, sorrow and fear into joy and love:

Oh, blessed work for Jesus!
Oh, rest at Jesus' feet!
There toil seems pleasure,
My wants are treasure,
And pain for Him is sweet.

(GH 26.5)

The only requirement is that the believer surrender his will totally to the deity, the latter taking control. Frances Havergal's popular "Take my life and let it be / Consecrated, Lord, to Thee" (GH 124 and 663) is representative in that it lists all the items one devotes to the service of Jesus—feet, hands, lips, life, etc. A similar approach is that of Theodore Monod's hymn, "All of self, and none of Thee." It begins as follows:

Oh the bitter pain and sorrow
That a time could ever be
When I proudly said to Jesus
"All of self, and none of Thee."
(GH 149.1)

Succeeding verses tell how Jesus "found" him, how he saw Jesus's suffering, and how the deity's "tender mercy" brought him around to "less of self, and more of Thee," until finally the hymn concludes:

Higher than the highest heavens,
Deeper than the deepest sea,
Lord, Thy love at last has conquered
"*None* of self, and *all* of Thee."
(GH 149.4)

An even more graphic portrayal appears in "A Sinner Forgiven," a story-type hymn in which the woman of Luke 7:37 comes "to the hall of the feast" to ask forgiveness of Jesus:

She heard but the Saviour; she spoke but with sighs;
She dare not look up to the heav'n of His eyes;
And the hot tears gush'd forth at each heave of her breast,
As her lips to His sandals were throbbingly pressed.
(GH 44.3)

In each case, whatever the varieties of portrayal, the message is clear: surrender, emotion, and intimacy, as well as passivity, are at the center of the salvation process. The intensity of passion and surrender increases as one moves from earlier hymnals to later ones. By the time of *Gospel Hymns,* the concern with emotions has changed from a general portrayal of the "heart" as the problem, to a strong focus on the person of Jesus as source of emotional strength. That is reflected in the hymn themes, which show that *Gospel Hymns* has more hymns devoted to the theme of "Jesus as loving and beloved" than to any other single category.

Passivity and passion, I would argue, are the two strategic foci of the gospel hymn collection. This appears in various ways at the level of metaphors as well as in the dominant themes. In the classes of metaphors described earlier in this chapter, we find that the dominant ones are in accord with the passivity/passion categories. The first, negative versus positive emotions, clearly reflects the portrayal of individuals and the deity in terms of the emotions or passions. The second, turmoil versus rest, articulates passivity in the face of chaotic forces, as I have shown at length above. The third, weakness versus strength, underscores what I observed in the pages immediately preceding: the human being as dependent on Jesus for strength; surrendering with all one's human weaknesses, and then being transformed by reliance on Jesus. As the child's Sunday school song goes: "Little ones to him belong; they are weak but He is strong. / Yes, Jesus loves me. . . . " There is virtually no difference between this and the approach of the gospel hymns, except of course that the latter were not only for children. This complex of images—the first three categories in the list—accounts for nearly two-thirds of all the metaphors in the gospel hymns. The only other large category is that of guilt versus atonement which, as we have seen, was inherited from an earlier era and by the late nineteenth century had undergone sharp decline and considerable transformation.

The thematic analysis also supports the proposed interpretation. Themes suggestive of hierarchy, active agency, legal mediation have declined; those of grace, refuge, a loving Jesus, and a happy heaven have become central—again, nearly two-thirds of all the hymns. Only two themes of significant frequency might raise questions about this general interpretation, namely hymns of battle and hymns of mission. How can those fit into a scheme which emphasizes passivity, since both sorts of hymns seem to imply active Christian agents trying to exert some power over the world, either to conquer evil forces or to convert the heathen? This is an important question, not so much because of the number of such hymns—there are eighteen hymns classified as battle hymns, and forty-one in the missionary category—but because of the popularity of some, out of proportion to their numbers. The battle hymns, for example, include such stellar examples as Sabine Baring-Gould's "Onward, Christian Soldiers" (GH 87 and 365) and P. P. Bliss's "Hold the Fort" (GH 11). The latter was supposed to have been inspired by a story told by Whittle about Sherman's march to the sea, so that a Civil War legend combined with Bliss's own legend to make it one of the most popular hymns of the Moody-Sankey era.[15] The missionary hymns again include many well-known ones; in addition, they had the added advantage of being used at meetings of voluntary societies engaged in missions or social reform work, besides at the revival meetings proper. In any case, the preeminence of the missionary cause in nineteenth-century evangelicalism requires some consideration of this type of hymn.

First, the battle hymns. One would expect them to be hymns of conquest, especially given the example of "Onward, Christian Soldiers, marching as to war." In fact Baring-Gould's portrayal of the Christian battle is atypical; most battle hymns are not those of the conquistador. Two of them (GH 429 and 518) concentrate more on the kingly role of Jesus than on the battle itself; and most of the rest portray not a conquering army, but rather bands of fighters exhorted to "stand," "display" the banner, be "firm" and "steady," "not turn away" (GH 69.3, 381, 357, 652). "Hold the Fort" itself, as the title suggests, is primarily that kind of hymn:

> Ho! my comrades, see the signal
> Waving in the sky!
> Reinforcements now appearing
> Victory is nigh!
>
> See the mighty host advancing
> Satan leading on:
> Mighty men around us falling,
> Courage almost gone.
>
> CHORUS:
> "Hold the fort, for I am coming,"
> Jesus signals still,
> Wave the answer back to heaven,
> "By Thy grace we will."
>
> (GH 11.1–2, Ch)

The army is on the defensive, waiting to be saved by the action of Jesus, but not going out to conquer territory. In other hymns militant phrases occur, like Baring-Gould's "Like a mighty army moves the Church of God" (GH 87.2), but more often aggressive movement is attributed to the enemy: "the mighty host advancing," as above, or "many giants, great and tall, / Stalking thro' the land"

(GH 652.3). The Christian army usually waits in a "leaguered camp" for the "night alarm" (GH 354.3)—clearly a defensive rather than an offensive militia. The language of the battle hymns is, therefore, ambivalent on the active/passive scale.

Interestingly, much the same turns out to be true of the typical missionary hymn. The early nineteenth century provides examples of hymns which express an aggressive activism, but this type does not remain prominent. The classic instance is Lowell Mason's "Missionary Hymn," with lyrics written in 1819 by the English Bishop of Calcutta, Reginald Heber:

From Greenland's icy mountains, from India's coral strand,
Where Afric's sunny fountains roll down their golden sand,
From many an ancient river, from many a palmy plain,
They call us to deliver their land from error's chain.

What tho' the spicy breezes blow soft o'er Ceylon's isle,
Tho' every prospect pleases and only man is vile?
In vain, with lavish kindness, the gifts of God are strown:
The heathen, in his blindness, bows down to wood and stone.

Shall we, whose souls are lighted by wisdom from on high,
Shall we to men benighted the light of life deny?
Salvation! oh, salvation! The joyful sound proclaim
Till earth's remotest nation has learned Messiah's name.
(GH 41.1–3; also Lyre 17, H&M 59)

The text embodies the older themes of natural man being a rebel, being "vile" and in "error"; but more, it is a prototype of nineteenth-century imperial religion. Mission is equated with ideological conquest. Those lighted with wisdom triumphantly carry their ideas to other lands, and bear them down upon other, "benighted" peoples. Mission means spreading out from the center—

always Britain or America, in English hymns—over the entire globe.[16]

Several post-1820 gospel hymns still copy that mode, but most of the missionary hymns exhibit a different approach—not imperial mission, but "rescue mission." The dominant metaphor is not the spread of empire but the gathering in of harvest or, alternatively, the rescue of shipwrecked sailors, as in Dwight L. Moody's description of his calling: "God has given me a lifeboat and said, 'Moody, save all you can!' " "Scattering seeds of kindness" and "bringing in the sheaves," Christian workers do not move far from their territory; at most, they "throw out the lifeline" (GH 86, 609, 441). They are shepherds, who try to bring others into the fold and keep them from straying:

> "Call them in"—the poor, the wretched,
> Sin-stained wand'rers from the fold.
> (GH 72.1)

Or, to quote again from Fanny Crosby's hymn:

> Rescue the perishing,
> Care for the dying,
> Snatch them in pity from sin and the grave;
> Weep o'er the erring one,
> Lift up the fallen,
> Tell them of Jesus the mighty to save.
> (GH 592.1)

Such hymns reveal that the shift from a more active to a more passive conception of the religious life affected the idea of mission as well. Christians do not attempt to impose their will on the world, but rather sit down—for example, in a "settlement house"—in the midst of it, and invite sinners to come in: "Plead with them earnestly, / Plead with them gently: / He will forgive if they only believe" (GH 592.2). Yet the notion of passive mission can be and is pushed still further, reaching its logical conclusion in hymns in which Christians say and do nothing, but are simply lights shining in the darkness. That type of expression is known from the Sunday-school song, "This little light of mine, / I'm gonna let it shine," but its best representative in *Gospel Hymns* is Bliss's "Let the Lower Lights Be Burning," still a favorite among singers of traditional gospel hymns:

Brightly beams our Father's mercy
From His lighthouse evermore,
But to us He gives the keeping
Of the lights along the shore.

Dark the night of sin has settled,
Loud the angry billows roar;
Eager eyes are watching, longing,
For the lights along the shore.

Trim your feeble lamp, my brother:
Some poor sailor tempest-tost,
Trying now to make the harbor,
In the darkness *may be lost.*
CHORUS:
Let the lower lights be burning!
Send a gleam across the wave!
Some poor fainting, struggling seaman
You may rescue, you may save.

(GH 45)

That hymn would totally dispel the notion that saving people from a shipwreck might be a strenuous task. Again, people passively tossed about by the forces of chaos are rescued, brought into the circle of salvation by another passive force, the "lights along the shore."

We can elaborate on the import of such themes by turning to the third dimension chosen for analysis: the forms of the hymns, as articulated most clearly in their modes of address. In this regard, the hymnals exhibit striking differences. The proportion of hymns addressed to the deity drops sharply as we proceed from Watts and Wesley to *Gospel Hymns.* Further, whereas most of that category in Watts were hymns of praise or thanksgiving, those are much less prominent in Sankey's hymnal. The hymn of praise in Watts might be, typically, the following:

Now for a tune of lofty praise
To great Jehovah's equal Son!
Awake my voice in heav'nly lays,
Tell loud the wonders he hath done.
(Watts 43.1)

In the gospel hymns, the address to the deity has changed to the soft supplication of Fanny Crosby:

Pass me not, O gentle Savior,
Hear my humble cry;
While on others Thou art smiling,
Do not pass me by.
(GH 585.1)

The shift from praise to prayer is unmistakable; and it provides, as we shall see below, an important clue to understanding the more general changes in hymnody.

Another noteworthy change is in the proportion of hymns of exhortation, much greater in Sankey than in Watts. That might be expected in the movement from Puritanism to revivalism, as an increasingly missionary and evangelical attitude develops, exhorting sinners to convert and Christians to work to convert them. Yet most of the gospel hymns fall under the category neither of invocation nor exhortation; they are primarily descriptive, affirmative, addressed to no audience in particular. That sort of hymn is well represented in all the hymnals; but its extraordinary predominance in the gospel hymns (and in the *Lyre*) must be accounted for.

Such hymns, which describe personal experience or tell a story (often from the Bible) might be a substitute for a creedal affirmation, as Horton Davies has suggested for the hymns of Nonconformist worship in England.[17] That interpretation, however, is inadequate for the American case because it does not consider the revivalistic context of the gospel hymns and the otherwise extraordinary shift in forms from Watts (whose hymns of affirmation are much closer to being creeds). The descriptive hymns, like creeds, affirm and glorify the deity, heaven, and the Christian life but they are often implicitly addressed to a human audience. The hymn entitled "Home of the Soul" may serve as an example. It is primarily an affirmation, but it begins with a reference to an anonymous "you," and the description of heaven is laced in the third and fourth verses with an implicit invitation to "meet me there":

I will sing you a song of that beautiful land,
The far away home of the soul,
Where no storms ever beat on the glittering strand,
While the years of eternity roll.

Oh, that home of the soul in my visions and dreams,
Its bright jasper walls I can see;
Till I fancy but thinly the vail intervenes
Between the fair city and me.

That unchangeable home is for you and for me,
Where Jesus of Nazareth stands,
The King of all kingdoms forever, is He,
And He holdeth our crowns in His hands.

Oh, how sweet it will be in that beautiful land,
So free from all sorrow and pain;
With songs on our lips and with harps in our hands,
To meet one another again.
(GH 15; repetitions omitted)

That hymn is quite typical in being primarily descriptive, but slipping in surreptitiously, as it were, an invitation to conversion. A hymn like "I Love to Tell the Story" is another example, with only one aside to the audience in the second verse:

I love to tell the Story of unseen things above,
Of Jesus and His glory, of Jesus and His love!
I love to tell the Story! Because I know it's true;
It satisfies my longings, as nothing else would do.

I love to tell the Story! More wonderful it seems,
Than all the golden fancies of all our golden dreams.
I love to tell the Story! It did so much for me!
And that is just the reason, I tell it now to thee.
(GH 30.1–2)

In fact, the hymn never gets around to telling the story, but only talks about telling one. Hymns like this emphasize the setting of an exchange between people, and thereby imply some other role than simply creedal affirmation or its analogue.

This form can best be understood as a "testimony." It is an eyewitness description, so to speak, of various dimensions of the revivalist drama of salvation, putting on record what the witness has "seen" or experienced. If the scenario of the older hymns was that of a criminal pleading before God with Christ as his advocate, that of the gospel hymns is one of Jesus on trial before a huge, anonymous, and largely hostile jury, with happy Christians appearing on the witness stand in his behalf.[18] They describe the character and actions of the accused in glowing detail, celebrate his great deeds, ask others to consider his suffering and extend their sympathies, and finally plead for his acceptance into their hearts.

The notion of "witnessing" finds confirmation in other aspects of the hymn language. The hymns often use verbs of witnessing: "I saw," "I hear," "I remember." "Home of the Soul," quoted above, elaborates the theme, speaking of "visions and dreams" in which the singer is a witness to the glories of heaven itself. Indeed in many of the hymns, to become a Christian means to become a witness, a viewer if not a voyeur, as in the following verse by Bliss:

> Look unto Me and be ye saved,
> I heard the Just One say;
> And as by faith on Him I gazed,
> My burden rolled away.
>
> (GH 238.1)

Such an account of salvation is characteristic of the gospel hymn testimonies.

We find, then, some distinctive and mutually reinforcing patterns in the gospel hymns collected by Ira Sankey. They portray human beings as passive victims, tossed about in an evil world; saved by passive, passionate, and almost erotic surrender to an equally passive deity. The hymns focus on the emotional life, in which Christians pour out their hearts in supplication, join with Jesus in intimate union, and share their experiences by witnessing to one another. One quotation from the hymnal itself encapsulates this rhetoric. Appearing as an epigraph to hymn No. 333 by evangelist Major D. W. Whittle, it is a fragment from a work by the British evangelical preacher

Charles Spurgeon: "I looked to him, he looked on me, and we were one for ever." "Looking" as a description of the salvation event suggests both passivity and the act of witnessing. "I looked to him" expresses the dependence of the devotee on Jesus in prayer, supplication, and surrender, while "he looked on me" can stand for Jesus's benevolent concern and love for human beings. "We were one for ever" reminds us of the intimate union characteristic of the relation between the deity and his devotees. And the epigraph itself is, of course, a testimonial. The epigraph does not show the other side of the picture, the pre-salvation human condition: restlessness, turmoil, wandering, darkness, sorrow, agony—all of which the hymns vividly portray as well. Yet it does provide a kind of capsule summary of the salvation process according to gospel hymn rhetoric.

We can now formulate more precisely our questions about the gospel hymns. Why gospel hymns? becomes, why *this* sort of language? How and why did these developments come about: the move from worm to wanderer; from guilt to turmoil; from Christ the Clarence Darrow of the heavens to Jesus our secret confidant; from imperial mission to rescue mission; from praise to prayer and testimony? The sweeping generalizations to which we are too well accustomed—social change, intellectual reorientation, retreat from the world, pessimism—fall ponderously upon the ear in the face of such specific questions about changes in religious rhetoric. The questions can be answered, however; in fact they give their own clues to an explanation in the history of revivalism itself, as we will see in the chapters that follow.

3

Passion and Order: The Problem of Social Religion

ANALYSIS of the gospel hymn lyrics, as an exercise in elementary rhetorical criticism, makes it possible to isolate the most important components of form and content in that language system. To uncover the deeper significance of those features and of the system as a whole, we must place them in specific linguistic and social contexts. Fortunately, we can do that for our materials with considerable precision by looking to the history of Northern revivalism in the nineteenth century. It is most fruitful to begin with the fact noted in the last section of the preceding chapter, that the gospel hymns' modes of address emphasized prayers of supplication, testimony, and exhortation over the older praise forms. For when we examine revivalist practice, we find that there emerged an increased interest in prayer, testimony, and exhortation from the time of the revivals in upstate New York led by Charles Grandison Finney in the mid-1820s.[1] By referring to some of the important literature on those practices, we can begin to elucidate the significance of the *forms* which were to dominate the gospel-hymn tradition.

Prayer, testimony, and (lay) exhortation can best be understood as the basic forms of what I will call "social religion," a new complex of religious practices which dissolved the earlier Puritan distinction between private and public religious exercises. In the Puritan tradition, conversion was a private experience, shared directly only with one's intimates (so that a father might take responsibility for accounting for the religious state of his children and his wife) and, if one's church required a relation of experience for membership, with the elders of the church. But even when the private religious life was linked to the church by means of the conversion narrative, the private "exercises" of religion were still carefully distinguished from the public ones which centered on the Sabbath services and other fully "public" meetings. The nineteenth-century explosion of revivalism, however, introduced a great variety and quantity of other religious meetings, from the "protracted meetings" of the revivals themselves to many small group gatherings for devotions, for discussion of biblical exegesis, theology, or morals, and for the sharing of religious experiences. These "social religious meetings," as they were often called, had their precursors in the Puritan system, just as testimony was an outgrowth of the narration of the conversion experience, and as prayer was a familiar part of both public and private worship. Further, there may well have been influential forerunners in other traditions, for example in Methodism with its practice of "class meetings." Nevertheless, the ascendancy of these new forms in the context of Northern revivals was, in the United States, clearly a nineteenth-century phenomenon. The growth of social religion embodied a novel approach to religious practice and a new set of conceptual tools for understanding the religious life of the individual and its relationship to society as a whole.

Preeminent among the newly developing concepts was an elaborate terminology based on notions about the feelings or affections—again, developing out of the conversionist language inherited from Puritanism, but now applied in the *social* context of revivals. It is clear from the available literature that prayer, testimony, and exhortation were employed to create a *community* of intense *feeling,* in which individuals underwent similar experiences (centering on conversion) and would thenceforth unite with others in matters of moral decision and social behavior. The language employed in such contexts laid the foundation for the description of human beings and their relations to God or Jesus in terms of their emotions, a feature which we have observed in the gospel hymns. The intense intimacy of that language, articulated in a communal context, reflects new practices which became prominent in the Finney revivals; and the fervent debates over those practices reveal just how novel and tentative they were. Indeed, after Finney's revivals in New York, the issue of *control* of intense emotion became central in the attempt to make social religion a workable source of order. The problem of the passions in society was not immediately solved. It was not until evangelicals began to develop the rhetoric of domesticity that they arrived at a viable conceptualization of emotions and sociality, as we will see in Chapters 4 and 5. But that is to anticipate the argument too far. We must first examine the debates over the forms of social religion and show how they are relevant to understanding the forms of the gospel hymns.

Especially illuminating in this context are the minutes of the 1827 New Lebanon (New York) conference, at which the "Western" revivalists or Finneyites met the "Eastern" evangelicals led by Lyman Beecher, at a meeting designed to bring the two parties to an agreement on the "new measures" then employed by some revivalists.[2] None of the ministers in attendance was against revivals as such; indeed Beecher along with Asahel Nettleton and others had been largely responsible for fashioning the revival into an instrument of evangelical order in the New England churches. The preface to the minutes of the New Lebanon meeting assured readers that none "doubted the reality and unspeakable importance of these refreshings, or had ceased to pray that they might become coextensive with the earth; for here, let the enemy [primarily the Unitarians] know, there has been perfect unanimity"; and the conference began with unanimous votes on the appropriateness of revivals of religion and the use of human agency therein.[3] Where the parties differed was on the propriety of certain kinds of behavior evidenced by those human agents. Both sides brought to the conference table resolutions regarding permissible behavior, of which one contained an oblique reference to testimony and several dealt directly with prayer.

The practice of testimony was apparently well accepted and its "rules" understood, for the only reference to it was in a proposal by the Easterners which stated: "Those meetings for social religious worship, in which all speak according to their own inclinations, are improper; and all meetings for religious worship ought to be under the presiding influence of some person or persons."[4] The motion was immediately voted unanimously in the affirmative. Testimony by this time must have been a subsidiary problem. Finney devoted one lecture in his 1835 *Lectures on Revivals of Religion* to the matter of "testifying" for God, but he did not treat testimony extensively as a distinct form. For him, testifying had primarily to do with living an exemplary life, not just talking about it and admonishing or exhorting others. Yet that suggests that telling of conversions and exhorting others was a common practice, and that testifiers were regarded by others as models to be imitated. The "looks and lives and warnings" of the converted—their testimony and exhortation—"all tend to promote the conversion of their impenitent friends," Finney said.[5] He raised no question bout it, nor did he defend it; he only warned that it might become mere talk with no action to support it.

That perspective was not peculiar to Finney; the other side held much the same view of testimony in the work of conversion. William Sprague, an anti-Finney man who identified himself with the prestigious orthodox tradition of Jonathan Edwards, Timothy Dwight, and Nathaniel Taylor, spoke a few words in defense of such practices in his lectures on revivals, published in 1832 under the same title as Finney's.[6] Although it had not always been the practice, he said, it was now well accepted that "private Christians" have a great deal of work to do in a revival in terms of "counsel and instruction" to awakened sinners; and indeed the influence of "example" was one of the means used by the Holy Spirit to bring sinners to the point of conviction, operating by means of "sympathy" or correspondence of feeling.[7] That, as we will see, was a crucial notion. For the present it suffices to observe that both sides apparently used something resembling testimony and may have permitted lay exhortation as well. Certainly such practices became widespread in the development of evangelical reform societies, most notably in the later antislavery and temperance organizations.[8] If in fact there was general agreement on such practices, one may ask why the New Lebanon conference brought up the matter at all. The resolution against "all speaking according to their own inclinations" signals a concern for the *way* the testimony and exhortation might be used, a concern for decorum, control, and proper leadership in orchestrating "sympathy" and "feeling" to bring others to conversion. The Easterners apparently were worried that such behavior might get out of hand, even with such an otherwise innocuous practice of lay people telling of their experiences.

The issue of prayer involved much greater difficulties between the two camps, and is proportionately more illuminating with regard to the issue of order and emotion. The first resolution which split the conference stated, 'In social meetings of men and women, for religious worship, females are not to pray." The Easterners also proposed that "audible groaning, violent gestures, and boisterous tones, in prayer, are improper." That resolution was amended twice and finally passed in the form, "audible groaning in prayer, is in all ordinary cases, to be discouraged; and violent gestures, and boisterous tones, in the same exercise, are improper." Finally, a most interesting set of distinctions emerged in an apparently lengthy argument involving different contexts for prayer—public, social, and private. It is worth quoting at length from the minutes:

> Mr. Edwards [an Easterner] introduced the following proposition:
>
> "The calling of persons by name in prayer ought to be carefully avoided."
>
> The motion was seconded, and after some discussuon, it was moved and seconded that it be so amended as to read as follows:
>
> "The calling of persons by name in social circles for prayer ought to be carefully avoided." This amendment did not prevail.
>
> Mr. Edwards moved that the proposition be so amended as to read as follows:
>
> "The calling of persons by name in social prayer ought to be carefully avoided."
>
> The motion was seconded, and the amendment prevailed.
>
> Mr. Lansing [a Westerner] then moved that the proposition be so amended as to read as follows:

> "The calling of persons by name in public prayer ought to be carefully avoided."

That last amendment barely passed, after an argument over whether the moderator was allowed to vote; the final vote was affirmative, but the reintroduction of the previous proposition failed to achieve a general consensus.[9] Indeed, it is clear from the minutes, which report people abstaining and apparently disappearing from the meeting, that those in attendance were far from satisfied. The above excerpt shows some troubling issues and some neat parliamentary maneuvers—as when Lansing shifted the discussion to *public* prayer in order to avoid a vote on *social* prayer—which indicate that important matters were at stake. We must examine the issue of of prayer more closely in order to determine why that was the case.

Fortunately, we know something about the type of prayer that was involved not only from observers' descriptions, as of people "groaning" in prayer, but also from Finney himself. In his 1835 *Lectures* he went to some lengths to describe and justify the practice of the "prayer of faith," also called "effectual prayer" or "prevailing prayer." The importance of the matter may be judged by the fact that he devoted five of the twenty-two lectures to prayer—four to the prayer itself and one to the holding of prayer meetings.[10] Clearly, even in those lectures where he had modified his earlier, more radical stance, it was a crucial matter for him as well as his critics. The theory, of course, was developed after the fact, but it was so closely entwined with the actual practice, and so influential in defining future revivalist practice, that it is an excellent resource in our effort to interpret the meaning of prayer in this and later periods of revivalism.

The essence of the prayer of faith, Finney declared, was that it achieved its object. Prayer from the right motives, in accordance with God's providences and promises and the Holy Spirit's guidance, presented for a definite object by one who had renounced all sin—that kind of prayer would prevail with God. There were some difficulties with such a notion, since it was presumed that God acted on his own will in such matters, and the prayer of faith seemed to assume that human beings could change his mind. Finney responded to such criticism by claiming that the effect was rather to change the feelings of men, so that it would be right for God to do for them what otherwise he could not have properly done but wanted to do anyway. Within even a moderately predestinarian framework, the logic was tortuous; and it usually ended with an assertion that those who haven't experienced it could not begin to understand such a high level of spirituality.[11]

The point of the whole exercise, however, really had nothing to do with cause and effect relations between people and God as those were narrowly understood. Rather, the problem with which it was designed to deal was that of the Christian's "state of mind" or, as Finney had said, with changing people's *feelings*. All his descriptions of the practice of prayer—and to these portions he devoted much more time than to obvious requirements like its performance in the name of Christ, scripturally, and from right motives—emphasized the intensity of experience. The petitioner was "bold" in importuning God, persevering, strong in desire even to the point of agony (Finney sometimes called it "agonizing prayer") and great "travail of soul." The mind and emotions were to be totally focused on the object of prayer until, whether after hours or weeks, God brought rest and relief in the promise of an answer to the prayer. Such intense mental concentration and pouring out of one's desires often involved violent gesticulation and other bodily activity (the "violent gestures" and "boisterous tones" which annoyed the Easterners at New Lebanon). But more important, according to Finney, was the role of this kind of prayer in creating a particular atmosphere, a kind of community of feeling between God and the individual and, when carried out in prayer meetings, with the entire congregation. For in the prayer of faith, Finney said, the Holy Spirit "prays for us, by exciting our faculties"; there is created "a bond of union between Christ and the Church"; one is brought into "sympathy" with God; and it "cements the hearts of Christians" one to another.[12] Prayer results in a sort of communal union, defined in terms of a common feeling or excitement of mental faculties brought about by the Holy Spirit. Just as in the case of testimony, we find here a strong accent on likeness of feeling in the religious meeting.

Finney had previously taken up the matter of likeness of feelings in his controversial sermon, "Christian Affinity," on the text of Amos 3:3: "Can two walk together except they be agreed?"[13] Preached early in 1827 in the heat of the debates over the revivals, but published later, it argues for an understanding of divisions among people as based on similarities and differences in the feelings or affections.

> For two to be agreed, implies something more than to be agreed in *theory*, or in understanding; for we often see persons who agree in theory,. . . . but who differ vastly in *feeling and practice*. . . . Saints and sinners often embrace in theory the same religious creed, while it is plain that they differ widely in feeling and practice.
>
> We have reason to believe that holy angels and devils apprehend and embrace *intellectually* the same truths, and yet how very differently they are affected by them.
>
> These different effects, produced in different minds by the same truths, are owing to the different state of the *heart* or *affections* of the different individuals.[14]

To Finney that was one of the basic "laws of the mind," to which he often adverted in appealing to audiences. In the case at hand, he went on to apply it to the situation of Christians. First taking examples from politics, he argued that one could talk favorably about a subject to a politician who enjoys it, and he would be delighted; but if you "change your style and tone—let down your fire and feeling—turn the subject over—present it in a drier light," then he would be displeased. Or in the case of music, if one is in a melancholy mood, one likes plaintive tunes and will turn away from marching music. So the case is the same in religious matters:

> Your heart is glowing with religious feelings. . . . Suppose you hear a cold man *preach* or *pray*; while he remains cold, and you are warm with feeling, you are not interested, for your affections are not fed and cherished unless the comes up to your tone. . . . Suppose you are lukewarm, and carnal and earthly in your affections; you hear one exhort, or pray, or preach, who is highly spiritual and fervent and affectionate; if you cling to your sins, and your affections will not rise; if, through prejudice, or pride, or the earthly and sensual state of your affections, you refuse to kindle and to grasp the subject, although you admit every word he says, yet you are not *pleased*. He is above your temperature; you are annoyed with the *manner* and fire and spirit of the man.[15]

People in similar states of feeling, in short, would "walk together," would be agreed; if they were Christians, one could speak of "Christian affinity." Contrariwise, those who differed in their hearts and affections would disagree. Thus the "lukewarm professors" often had difficulty, Finney said, with the use of "means" in revivals and the "manner" of preaching or praying, because they were not up to the "temperature" of the "conversation."

The point is clear: those who opposed the revivals were simply too "cold" to appreciate them. Most of the sermon is devoted to elaborating that point and comparing the opposition stirred up by Finney to (of course) that occasioned by Jesus and his apostles in the early days of Christianity. Replying, for example, to those who had charged him with stirring up only "animal feeling," Finney retorted that since all people had animal feeling in common, all would be equally stirred by a preacher who appealed only to it: "they will all weep and seem to melt, and no one will be offended, and I may add, no one will be convicted or converted."[16] Since his preaching caused offense, he therefore was appealing to more than just animal feeling. Such a heads-I-win-tails-you-lose argument outraged Finney's opponents, of course.[17] But what is more important for our purposes is to notice how Finney used the categories of feeling, of the "affections," in his attempt to make social groupings and religious affiliations intelligible. Feelings for him were at the basis of social affinities; indeed, Finney seems to have had complete confidence that the feelings of people, once converted, could provide the entire basis of order in a godly community. Those who *felt* alike would agree and would act in concord. And social prayer and testimony were means of creating like feelings.

Finney's rhetoric was not calculated to win friends from among his opponents. Yet behind his attacks and their counterattacks lay a considerable similarity in many of their ideas—so it would seem at first glance. As we have already seen in William Sprague, some of Finney's opponents used the same language in talking about the efficacy of revivals, emphasizing concepts like "sympathy" and "fellow-feeling" in connection with testimony as example for others. As Sprague went on to say, when Christians in a meeting are filled with a "deep, though silent anxiety," then

> every anxious countenance, every fixed eye, will preach; and it will utter a mysterious language that will not improbably waken up the sensibilities of the careless sinner; and this will naturally serve to open his ear to God's truth; and thus conviction may take the place of sympathy, and in the train of that may soon follow the clean heart and the right spirit.[18]

Such an understanding of feeling as a "mysterious language" with efficacious power was common among revivalists of all stripes. And in a similar vein, Beecher even admitted that perhaps a new theory of prayer might be appropriate for the church.[19] But that was as far as conciliatory gestures could go. The recognition of the operation of fellow-feeling through the example of "silent anxiety" and "fixed eyes" was quite different from approving of "audible groaning" and "violent gestures;" and according a greater importance to prayer was yet a long way from allowing females to pray in mixed company while petitioners prayed aloud for others by name.

The question was one of order and decorum, and perhaps ministerial control of revivals as well. Yet issues of order and decorum often run deep and should not be taken lightly.[20] That is the case here: as the anti-Finneyites sensed, a religion which allows such scope to feeling and emotion was a set of forms quite different from what they had known and encouraged. They saw it as the breakdown of all order, morality, and civilization, as Lyman Beecher argued in a letter written to N. S. Beman (a Finneyite) before the New Lebanon conference, appealing to him to change his practice. It was later published in, among other places, the London *Christian Observer*.[21] Beecher put forward his objections to Finney's revivals one by one, on the basis of his own understanding of proper social order. On the matter of female prayer, for example, he argued that praying in public distorts the sensibilites and therefore the moral character of women—with actresses as the leading example of such corruption:

> There *is* generally, and *should* be always, in the female character, a softness and delicacy of feeling which shrinks from the notoriety of a public performance. It is the guard of female virtue, and invaluable in its soothing, civilizing influence on man; and a greater evil, next to the loss of conscience and chastity, could not befal the female sex, or the community at large, than to disrobe the female mind of these ornaments of sensibility, and clothe it with the rough texture of masculine fibre. . . . and, if we need further testimony, the general character of actresses is a standing memorial of the influence of female elocution before public assemblies.[22]

That excerpt hints at the connection between "sensibilities," morality, etiquette, and civilization. But Beecher made the point even more explicit in his passionate summary:

> Should we therefore, in our zeal, strip religion of the mildness, and kindness, and courtesy of civilized decorum, and exhibit her in alliance with all the repellances and roughnesses of uncultivated humanity, as well might the bodies in the valley of vision have been animated and sent forth in all their deformity before the skin came upon them. True religion makes men courteous, and produces those salutary rules of civilized intercourse which distinguish Christian from savage nations.[23]

The practices of revival preaching and the events of the meetings violated such rules; and Beecher's vision of the expected results was little short of apocalyptic. They threatened, Beecher declared, to produce "civil war in the church, "dividing and distracting the churches by wrath, and strife, and endless divisions." Following on the heels of strife would come a decline in morals, for

> there is nothing so terrible and unmanageable as the fire and whirlwind of human passion, when once kindled by misguided zeal. . . . Like the cave of Aeolus, or the gate of Pandemonium, a single arm may suffice to let out the storm; but when once the atmosphere is put in motion, no human power can stop it, until it has exhausted its fury in works of moral desolation.

He runs through the litany once more: the threat of "semi-barbarism," "extravagance and disorder," the powerful "waters of human passion," and the prospect of moral desolation. All that, he concludes, stems from the revival meetings, whose great error is that of "pressing the mass of the community out of their place, and shaking together, in one cauldron of effervescence, all the passions of all the classes of human society."[24]

The metaphors communicate a great deal: Beecher's letter shows a far different evaluation of the role of emotion in revivals than appeared in Sprague's and Finney's lectures—a "cauldron of effervescence" contrasted with a gentle "sympathy." We can conclude that both evangelical camps viewed the passions or affections as profoundly important in conversion and in "cementing" the community, as Finney described it. But the older evangelicals also feared the power of the passions to break down the boundaries of groups or "classes" within a community. It should be noted that this was not simply a ministerial reaction to threats from lower social orders; the word "classes" did not usually mean socioeconomic or status groups (for that, "orders" or "ranks" was the preferred term). They were concerned at the mixing, "shaking together," and "pressing out of their place" of the various sorts of groups which were supposed to be separate and distinctive in their behavior—men and women, old and young, higher and lower. What was necessary to prevent this chaos, they thought, was a way of putting the passions into bounded form, in their "place," in proper contexts; they did not have Finney's confidence that emotions would organize themselves. Indeed the older evangelicals felt that they had ordered things quite well in the revival system they had devised over the previous two decades, but the Finneyites' carelessness in revivals was threatening that order. This is the issue at stake in the New Lebanon resolutions about decorum in worship and especially in the debate over social and public prayer: the issue of passions in their place. Public prayer, led by the minister in church, was no threat to an ordered community, but social prayer was a different matter. For the Finneyites, it served to cement together a broader community by generating "sympathy." In the eyes of Easterners like Beecher, it was potentially dangerous because it allowed emotions to spread wildly from group to group. The form of social prayer like that of testimony was to be preserved in popular hymnody and revivalism, but in the late 1820s it was a questionable practice.

Hymnody itself became a locus of similar debate during this period and the issues are closely related to those which emerged in arguments over prayer. It is important, first, to recognize that hymns were a relatively recent innovation in New England churches. The Puritans had at first not used hymns at all in their church services, but only the Psalms and occasionally other scriptural songs translated into English meter. As Cotton Mather wrote:

> The Churches of New-England admit not into their Publick Services, any other than the Psalms, Hymns and Spir-

> itual Songs, of the Old and New Testament, faithfully translated into English Metre. No, not so much as the, Te Deum; An Hymn which indeed is not mentioned by any Author more Ancient than the Rules which Old Benet wrote for his Monks, about the middle of the Sixth Century. . . . In this thing they agree to the Act of the Laodicean Synod; That no private Psalms be used in the Church. And they almost confine themselves unto the Limitations enjoined by the first Synod of Bracara, Let nothing be Sung in the Church, but the Psalms of the Old Testament.[25]

Mather allowed that "The private Companies & Families of the faithful . . . have sometimes employed what Verified Portions of Scripture and other devout Hymns they find for their Edification," but was emphatic about restricting congregational worship to psalmody.[26] That reflects a sharp distinction between the public and private modes of practice which had begun to erode by the nineteenth century. Even when Issac Watts's psalms and hymns were introduced in the early eighteenth century, they did not significantly alter the public/private dichotomy. Watts's reforms were designed primarily to make the content of psalmody more Christian (less Jewish) in its language and the whole "system of praise" better suited to the Puritan focus on the sermon. But he did not believe that the whole psalter or even all his hymns were suitable for *public* Sabbath worship.[27] Cotton Mather had concurred; on receiving a copy of Watts's *Hymns and Spiritual Songs*, he praised them in his diary and announced his plan to use them in family devotions, [28] that is, in the private sphere.

While it is probable that these careful distinctions were disrupted in the aftermath of the Great Awakening, the effects must have been local or temporary, for in New England the concern to maintain the boundaries between public and private appears only after the instituting of revivals at the very end of the eighteenth century and the first quarter of the nineteenth. Let us be clear about the distinctions which had to be negotiated. Public worship was the regular congregational meeting. Private exercises involved prayer and devotions of the individual—the "duties of the closet"—and also family devotions. It was in the matrix of private exercises that the conversion experience occurred, although one's struggle along the way could be shared with family members or church elders. When revivals became a regular feature of religious activity in New England after the turn of the century—and clearly by 1810 the leading New England churchmen were actively "revival men"—they were closely connected with devotional and study groups intended to maintain the level of piety and morality of the community. They were designed as a means of conversion, to enhance the churches, to provide spiritual discipline, and to ensure good order.[29] Revivals thus embodied a set of practices which bridged the (formerly private) experience of conversion and the communal activities of devotion, leading to church membership. They were clearly *social* practices, but not equivalent to the standard form of public worship. Yet if they were to contribute to social and moral order, they could not be allowed to get out of hand. An individual's perhaps extreme and ecstatic conversion experience could be potentially disruptive to a social meeting, as when a petitioner "groaned" and "agonized" aloud in prayer. Indeed, the New England evangelicals saw plenty of evidence of such dangers in the more raucous and emotional camp meetings which were becoming popular under influence from the West or perhaps, under their very noses, from urban Methodism.[30]

Correlatively, they worried about the vulgarizing influence of the folk hymns used in such revivals. Their response was to distinguish between songs for the revival itself as the locus of intense individual experiences, and hymns appropriate to the social meetings for prayer and devotion, where new converts joined with more experienced Christians. In 1821 a committee appointed by the General Association of Connecticut (Presbyterian and Congregationalist ministers) advocated the compilation of a respectable hymnal to be used as a supplement to Watts. The committee delayed in acting on the recommendation, but one of its members, Asahel Nettleton, went ahead on his own to produce *Village Hymns for Social Worship* (1824) which, although never officially authorized by the General Association, went through seven editions within three years. Nettleton used a variety of sources, including Watts, Charles Wesley, and John Newton—a leading eighteenth-century British composer who authored many pietistic-type hymns—but he explicitly rejected the popular revival hymns. Nettleton claimed that the latter were "ephemeral" and "utterly unfit for the ordinary purposes of devotion—as prescriptions, salutary in sickness, are laid aside on the restoration of health."[31] He thus implied that the intense conversion experiences of a revival were to be carefully separated from the "social worship" indicated by the book's title—the regular meetings for prayer, the "ordinary purposes of devotion." It was precisely that separation which was becoming increasingly difficult to maintain.

The issue became a matter of more pointed debate in the wake of Finney's revivals and the more intense New England revivals of the late 1820s. Beginning in 1830, a Connecticut pastor and supporter of Finney, Joshua Leavitt, began to publish in his revival weekly the *New York Evangelist* samples of revival hymns from a collection he planned to issue in monthly installments. The collection culminated in *The Christian Lyre* (1831), Part I (six months) of which immediately sold 18,000 copies. The entire collection went through eighteen editions in two years and was still selling in the early 1850s. Leavitt saw his work as much like Nettleton's, but going beyond it in providing more of the currently popular songs:

> Every person conversant with revivals must have observed that whenever meetings for prayer and conference assume a special interest, there is a desire to use hymns and music of a different character from those ordinarily heard in the church. Nettleton's Village Hymns in a good degree meets the first want. Jocelyn's Zion's Harp [an accompanying book of tunes] partially supplies the other. But both are felt to be incomplete, as they are wanting in many pieces, which have proved to be of great use in revivals.[32]

By inserting *revival* hymns and tunes into a collection designed for "meetings for prayer and conference," that is, for *social* worship, Leavitt was in effect breaking the boundaries which Nettleton's work had tried to maintain.

The reaction from the other side—for we see here again the lines drawn between the pro-Finney and anti-Finney camps—was immediate and far less polite. Thomas Hastings and Lowell Mason, who for some years had been devoting themselves to the reform and teaching of church music in accordance with European standards, issued *Spiritual Songs for Social Worship* in 1832. As with Nettleton's volume, the title specifying its purpose is significant for its accent on proper boundaries of behavior. In their preface, they claimed that recent compilers, that is, Leavitt, had degraded hymnody by borrowing tunes from "the current love songs, the vulgar melodies of the street, of the midnight reveler, of the circus and ballroom"; and that, while the newly converted or reawakened Christian, "coming suddenly into a new world of light and love," might express his emotions "in the rudest of strains," that was not the aim of the printed hymnal. It should rather cultivate the finer emotions and edify the Christian.[33] There are remnants here of Beecher's ideology about the connection between religion, proper sensibilities, and civilization. More important for our purposes is the stress upon the separation of the conversion experience from social worship, where the printed hymnal was used. The compilers also asserted that their work was not intended for regular church services: "in the larger and more dignified assemblies, psalmody will continue to hold its appropriate place."[34] The boundaries were thus made equally clear between social and public worship.

The churning out of alternative hymnals and the snide remarks in prefaces about the inadequacies and improprieties of other compilers are important because they make clearer what is only hinted in the parallel debates over the prayer of faith, social and public prayer. What was *private,* namely the emotion connected with the intense experience of conversion, was being ushered into the public sphere—or, more precisely, into the social sphere, and perhaps threatening the public one as well. Groaning and praying aloud for others or singing hymns in a lighter style were appropriate only for private worship or in carefully limited circles, according to the older New England churchmen. But in that respect they were only watching their own ideas explode before their eyes, for it was they who had created the arena of social religion. The system of revivals instituted by Nettleton and Beecher had entailed a network of meetings for group worship outside the church—devotional meetings, prayer groups, study groups—whose purpose was to ensure moral order by mutual support and example. As Sprague indicated, Christians had begun to take responsibility for each other's spiritual and moral well-being, and therefore to watch over the emotional lives of others, praying for them and exhorting them. The older evangelicals approved such practices as long as they remained within the proper context—small "social circles" which generally included people of the same sex, intimate friends or relatives in most cases or, alternatively, occupational or age-group classes.[35] But the expansion of the circle beyond those limits worried the older men. The practices of the Finneyites, with their emphasis on intensity of experience shared in a social context, allowed new converts to accuse established church members of coldness, youth to disdain their elders, and in general upset the system of deferential interaction which Beecher and others regarded as essential to the protection of proper sensibilities, morals, good order, and—according to Beecher's domino theory—civilization as a whole.

The realm of the social had become in their eyes a voracious monster, usurping the attention of Christians from both public and private spheres. William Sprague complained in his *Lectures* that the weekday meetings of the devotional societies tended to lead Christians to disregard the private "duties of the closet" in such a way as to "render one's Christian character sickly and inefficient." Correlatively, he warned that although it had become common to increase the number of social prayer meetings in revival seasons, they were still not to be exalted to equality with the "public exercises" of the Lord's Day.[36] Social prayer, testimony and lay exhortation in social meetings, and hymn-singing had become such persuasive forms of religious practice that they threatened to become the center of religion. The forms which articulated a community of feeling were becoming more important than the older forms. For the Finneyites, that was fine: they discerned the basis for *all* religion and morals in the social realm which spiraled out from the revival. Conversion established individuals in a particular kind of relationship with God, by virtue of which they were automatically members of a social company, alike in interests and feelings, who shared work and worship and together were set apart from non-Christians. Whereas for older evangelicals, the basis of order derived from a system of more or less "natural" classes based on sex, age, rank, or "station," and a network of departments of the Christian life (private, social, public), the Finneyites sliced the world in a different and more simplistic way: real Christians versus non-Christians, according to their *feelings.* Prayer, testimony, and the popular hymn were the appropriate forms in which those feelings could be articulated and known.

Or supposedly they could be known. The problem was, How in actuality could one distinguish between right and wrong feelings? The forms of social religion were ultimately to win the day: "Pass me not, O gentle Savior" would become a social prayer uttered by mass audiences, and "What a Friend we have in Jesus" would be their testimony to a hostile world. "Love after loneliness" and "bliss after agony" would become the formulas which articulated the dichotomy between Christians and non-Christians. But in the Finney period, it was not at all clear that calm, peace, and bliss were the outcome of the revivals. As Beecher's letter shows, he regarded them as stirring up wild passions, clearly wrong feelings. Nor was the concern over the passions limited to the activity of revivals themselves. Propriety in worship was a crucial issue, but there was another dimension as well, namely the moral behavior of a person in the larger social world. The evidence of a pure heart, according to evangelicals of the period, ought to appear in the proper social behavior and moral action of the Christian. Concern over this aspect of "social religion" came to sharp focus with regard to the "societies" and "associations" which were part of the great evangelical network of benevolence.

Social religion was not merely social worship, narrowly understood. It also included an expanding web of benevolent societies which, again, had originally been inspired largely by the work of Beecher and Nettleton. They and their fellow ministers, concerned about moral decline, the failure of party politicians to enforce statutes regulating moral behavior, and the general threat of "French infidelism" connected with Jeffersonian democracy, had formed in 1812 the Connecticut Society for the Reformation of Morals and Suppression of Vice. The group was designed to unite those citizens who felt strongly about moral issues such as intemperance and Sabbath-breaking, pledge them to good behavior, and act as a force of "moral opinion" (carefully distinguished from political opinion) which would serve to raise community standards and prod magistrates to enforce the existing laws. The Connecticut Moral Society served as prototype for later associations which similarly represented efforts of a moral elite to promote the general welfare and convert others to their cause. By 1830 there was a complex network of such societies, national in scope, with purposes ranging from Bible and tract distribution to temperance and African colonization, to missions and seamen's aid. They were intended to preserve good order by relying on the spiritual and moral discipline provided by conversion, and on the company of fellow Christians, operating without the coercive force of government.[37]

One might imagine that the societies would provide a framework for moral behavior which would solve the problem of how to discern right feelings and a pure heart: those who support the reform effort are true Christians; those who do not, are not. That was the reformers' assumption, but the argument resembles Finney's against his opponents—if you're affected by my preaching, you're truly converted; if you remain cold, you're not. In the case at hand, it was not at all clear to everyone that the reforms proposed by the benevolent societies were for the common good, and in the late 1820s and the 1830s, the societies came under heavy attack. The most extreme case was opposition to the American Antislavery Society, led by converts of Finney, which declared slavery to be not merely an evil but a sin which required immediate repentance and reform. Their doctrine of "immediatism" raised violent opposition in the form of riots and mob attacks on abolitionist speakers. What is interesting from our point of view is that the abolitionists were criticized not only for wrong views of the good of society, but also for the methods they had used. The society was, according to their opponents, a group of foreign agents, fanatics, and amalgamationists using methods of operation which were beyond the control of the citizenry, designed to "*inflame the passions of the multitude*." Abolitionists were compared to French revolutionaries, scheming Jesuits, and numerous other conspiracies which exploited popular excitement for evil ends. Further, they were flooding the mails with "incendiary literature" and had become a propaganda machine intent on the subtle but effective coercion of everyone, even women and children.[38]

The language is significant. The evangelical reformers assumed that a change of heart in conversion produced right feeling which would automatically produce correct moral behavior. The critics turned the argument on its head: since the behavior of the societies was (by their lights) wrong, the societies were misusing the passions, inflaming them, creating excitement and appropriating it for immoral aims. That kind of attack was not restricted to the antislavery movement. The Sunday-School Union was accused by the Pennsylvania legislature in 1828 of trying to become "dictators of conscience," while the Sabbatarian movement of 1828–29 increased anticlerical sentiment in many quarters on account of the clergy's supposed attempt to tyrannize over people's minds.[39] The whole range of benevolent societies, but especially the temperance movement, came under attack from the pen of a widely read Whig pamphleteer and conservative evangelical, Calvin Colton. A former Presbyterian minister and friend of revivals and reform, Colton turned on the societies after returning in 1836 from a four-year visit to England, publishing a lengthy tract entitled *Protestant Jesuitism.*[40] As his language is in many ways revelatory of the attacks on the societies, it is worth considering in some detail.

According to Colton, Jesuitism was exemplified in the Society of Jesus but was a perennial tendency in religion. It developed from a

> mysterious operation of the affections and passions, . . . when fanaticism blended with bigotry, beginning with a mixture of truth and error, . . . impels the mind alike and equally from the control of common sense and common uprightness, discharges it from the common obligations of society, and lodges it in a region without law to make law for itself.. . .[41]

That is, Jesuitism is the passions gone wild and overwhelming the mind, so that fanaticism supersedes one's ordinary sense of social obligations and propriety. According to him, the benevolent societies had become Jesuitical, even though they began from good intentions, when their leaders discovered their power and influence over the minds of their followers and began to use that power tyrannically. Moral and religious reformers especially were tempted to abuse their influence because they were "literally in the wind of passion, and will be seen to veer and run as circumstances and fresh impulses may impel. It is not principle, but feeling, that guides them."[42] The people they led were of course susceptible to such appeals:

> . . . So long as the popular mind is infected with the love and determination for excitement—and especially so long as the people are urged on by an organized corps of itinerating, artful, everywhere-present empirics,—in such a state of things, it is even possible to carry an unreasonable, unphilosophical theory by storm, against the sobriety and good sense of the community. The great public, busy about other matters and their private concerns, but finding gratification at intervals of repose in sympathizing with philanthropic projects, are always ready to be wrought upon by an adequate machinery.[43]

Here we see the concern over the passions or feelings, the popular tendency toward "excitement," which was characteristic of the older evangelicals. Significantly, it has been combined in Colton's work with a fear of strong leaders and organizations—an "organized corps" of leaders and a social "machinery" which manipulates those feelings.[44] Certainly, Finney had been accused of similar manipulation when his opponents charged him with arousing "animal feeling." Now those accusations extended to the nature of organization itself, to the companies of individuals gathered into societies.

Colton also made explicit connections between the societies and revivalism. In an 1836 tract he had already attacked the new revivalism for its use of "a new and specific moral machinery, or system of measures, to be employed and applied in connexion with the most startling and terrific appeals to the feelings and passions" which ultimately destroyed the intellect.[45] For him, the "new measures" were not mere means but terrible machinery.

In 1839, writing in *A Voice from America to England,* he declared that even such excitement was insufficient to satisfy Americans:

> The Americans like a fervent, not to say a hot, religion. . . .
>
> But the stirring power of religion in the primary assemblies of the people at camp-meetings, and in revivals, is not enough. This is only one, and a distinct mode of its operation. It is properly the devotional part, not of the closet, but of the public assembly. It is where the mind luxuriates in its religiously passive condition and revels in extatic joy, or writhes in agony, while acted upon by a singular and powerful combination and concentration of social and religious influence.
>
> But . . . denied participation in affairs of State, as a body . . . they [the revivalists] have entered a new field, formed associations, and opened subscriptions, for the conversion—in other words, for the conquest—of the world.[46]

In other words, the overwrought feelings generated at revivals were threatening the whole world through the operation of the benevolent associations. The societies had, according to Colton, "set up a gigantic religious power, systematized, compact in its organization, with a polity and government entirely its own, and independent of all control. It exists, indeed, in different forms or collateral branches, having no visible corporate connexion, but a common sympathy."[47] The associations had in effect formed a conspiracy, bound together by feeling ("sympathy"); its power was absolute, but secret and inaccessible.

Although Colton's critique runs to the extreme, his rhetoric is illuminating for the way he brings together a concern over man's emotional nature and fears of improper use of power. It is precisely congruent with the legislature accusing the Sunday-School Union (of all people) of being "dictators of conscience," or the anti-abolitionists worrying about the reformers "inflaming the passions of the multitude." And all of these run parallel to the concerns of evangelicals about the Finney revivals. In each case, "feeling" was conceived of as a real power loose in the world. It was Sprague's "mysterious language" which could effect conversions; it was Finney's "sympathy" which could bind this world to the heavenly one and unite sincere Christians. But it was also a mighty tide which could sweep over civilization, as in Beecher's letter, and a field of "mysterious operations" which could set up its own kind of government beyond the control of the state, as Colton feared.

Indeed, in the 1830s and 1840s, almost any cause could be attacked for the way it used the passions, especially if it tried to organize them. Clerics responded to anticlerical sentiment by declaring that politics was a breeding ground of excitement, popular clamor, and faction. For example, Francis Wayland, president of Brown University, in an 1830 address to the Sunday-School Union, praised the potential of the benevolent societies but warned against the dangers of politics:

> We have provided no checks to the turbulence of passion: we have raised no barriers against the encroachments of a tyrannical majority. Hence, the very forms [of democracy] which we so much admire, are at any moment liable to become an intolerable nuisance, the instruments of ultimate and remediless oppression. . . .
>
> I will not here ask, whether any thing has ever transpired within your recollection, in the history of our republic, at which a thoughtful man may tremble. I will not ask, whether, when the most momentous questions are at stake, it be customary to address the passions, or the reason and

> conscience of our fellow citizens. I will neither ask, whether he would not be considered a novice, who was credulous enough to believe a politician honest. . . . I will not ask, whether the most infamous want of principle, hath always obstructed the advancement of him, who hath made his yell heard in the deafening clamour of electioneering strife. . . . I refer to these things, Christian brethren, to remind you how inevitable is the result, if it be not arrested by the redeeming influences of Christianity.[48]

Mormons and Catholics were attacked as conspiracies on much the same grounds as Colton attacked benevolent societies: on the one hand they were a centrally controlled hierarchy unresponsive to the will of the people; and on the other they exploited human passions through the Mormon practice of polygamy or the Catholic convent and confessional which supposedly veiled illicit and immoral activities.[49] Such attacks and counterattacks reveal an extraordinary sensitivity to what, in the language of the day, were called "influences" and "impressions" upon the mind and emotions, influences especially powerful when they came through well-directed organizational efforts.

The benevolent societies had, admittedly, left themselves open to such attacks. In their more exuberant moments they presented themselves as part of a grand system of control, as Clifford S. Griffin has observed:

> The societies frequently stressed that all the organizations were part of a general crusade against evil. Their officers wrote of the "sisterhood" of benevolent societies; of those "great mills and manufacturing establishments of the City of God, all located on the banks of that great river of life, whose waters turn their ponderous wheels"; of a tree, the trunk and branches of which were the societies. Officers told of a benevolent system "beautiful as the harmonies of nature"; of the "great and good" work all the societies

> did; of the roles which each of the groups played in the great drama of saving souls.[50]

To the leaders and participants, the system was grand and beautiful; but comparing themselves to all-encompassing systems or to mills and factories or even to sisterhoods (were they like convents?) was a dangerous game to play in that individualistic era. And in response, many—including many evangelicals—turned away from the great national societies. As John Higham has observed, there were two choices in the great "maelstrom of excitement" which pervaded the Jacksonian era: one could either celebrate it or one could reassert the traditional institutions as means of controlling it.[51] Some turned to politics, many evangelicals supporting the Whig party.[52] Conservatives in religious matters returned to ecclesiology, reasserting denominational traditions, emphasizing the catechism in Sunday schools, commissioning denominational hymnals, and discouraging (or at least not encouraging) revivals.[53] Some did try to straddle the fence, supporting benevolent societies with reservations about organizations. For example, Leonard Woods, writing in the *American Biblical Repository* for 1837, defended the voluntary associations despite their faults. After surveying the dismal state of churches in the United States and abroad and commenting on their tendency to schism and anarchy, he denied that the remedy was tighter ecclesiastical organization, as some had suggested. Rather, the voluntary associations ought to be reformed and refined, but not abandoned. On the one hand, he argued against those who would have the evangelicals return to more narrowly defined activities:

> . . . Some men . . . are earnest advocates for movements which are simple, narrow, easily comprehended, and

> easily controlled. But . . . is it entirely certain, that if our national institutions should be sundered into a hundred independent societies, we should escape trouble? Would not jealousy, envy, and the other bad passions have a fine opportunity to reveal their tendencies in the provincial or State or county associations? Could we wholly exclude the demon of party if we had twenty-six home missionary institutions, instead of two or three?[54]

The passions, in other words, were just as much a problem in small organizations as in large. On the other hand, Woods warned against broader powers wielded by the churches:

> Some persons may regard these strange and revolutionary movements in the churches as a signal for the abandonment of voluntary societies, and the warmer embrace of ecclesiastical organizations. All things appear to be loose and disorderly. In every outbreak of popular or clerical violence, they see the necessity of some single, central, coercive power. . . . But . . . our civil constitutions are utterly inconsistent with any such dictatorial, metropolitan influence. . . . Charities are not to be ordered or enjoined. They will flow freely or not at all.[55]

In fact, Woods concluded, agents of churches would likely be prey to all the faults of voluntary associations; therefore people should continue to place their trust in the latter.

Yet it is clear that Woods had some difficulty in steering a course for the voluntary associations and the whole evangelical enterprise. He wanted it to be national but not churchly, wide-ranging but not tyrannical, voluntary but organized. The problem is symptomatic of the character of social religion as a whole. Organizationally, the societies were supposed to be totally voluntary, but they had to have direction from officers and leaders. They were supposed to operate by moral suasion, not by coercion or appeal to the baser passions; but given the impressionability of human beings and the vulnerability of their affections, where could one draw the line? Societies, like revivals, were supposed to be based on community of feeling; yet there were no criteria for deciding between right and wrong feelings except what seemed to "feel right." How was one to judge a society, its aims and methods? How was it possible to discern the genuineness of a conversion, the sincerity of a revivalist, the grace of God in an awakening? How could one keep prayer and worship within proper bounds when the feelings of individuals were unleashed in a group? What would happen to religious sensibilities if holy song were set to worldly tunes? If the affections held society together, and if they were perverted or corupted, what would happen to the order of the world? These were all related problems which concerned evangelicals of the period.

The evangelicals, beginning with Nettleton and Beecher and more definitively with Finney, had created an interpretation of the world and specifically of the social order in terms of the emotions: a rhetoric and practice and theory of the passions—in social prayer, testimony, hymnody, benevolent societies—over against the older interpretations of the structure of society. Yet soon they found themselves without decisive and widely acceptable criteria for applying their interpretations. The world seemed aflame with tumultuous passions, and yet any attempt to order and organize people's affections seemed to violate the basic principles of self-control underlying the spiritual experience of revivals and the voluntary system of associations. Events seemed to be made up of all emotion or all organization, all passion or all order; or they were united in a perverted way into a terrible conspiracy. There was simply no way of satisfactorily combining the two. The next two decades after 1835, when widespread revivals declined and the societies fell into a slump, were a period of searching for the right metaphors, the appropriate rhetoric and practice, to serve as a basis for the union of order and passion.[56] The forms of social religion—prayer, testimony, exhortation, and the beginnings of popular hymnody, all in the context of the increasingly interdenominational revival—were preserved as they continued to be successful, although restrained and local in scope. The duality between good and bad emotions provided the foundation for a dualistic worldview, such as we saw in the gospel hymns. Moreover, the hymns' portrait of a world in turmoil is a direct descendant of the world aflame with passion that Beecher, Colton, and others perceived. But before the evangelicals could appropriate those ideas they had to find a way to turn them inside out, as it were, and use them strategically against opponents. To do that, they first had to find a way of ordering their own passions, of finding images which would convey depth of feeling as well as control. They found the perfect source in the emerging ideology of domesticity: the images of home, mother, and family.

4

Passion in its Place: The Domestic Image

IN the last chapter we observed the emergence of a novel kind of evangelical rhetoric—a rhetoric of the passions, centered in a community of feeling—and a rush of counter-rhetoric which portrayed the world as aflame with passion, while the masses were vulnerable to the whims of fanatic leaders or conspiracies to subvert the mind. For our purposes, the sociology of this exchange can be described very generally in terms of the broad changes taking place in American society.[1] Especially as a result of the settlement of the West and the industrialization of the Northeastern cities, large portions of the Northern population were dislodged or dislodged themselves from familiar locales, stable community structures, and traditional roles. For most white males the emerging society provided a variety of new occupations and enterprises in which they could invest their energies. The responses to these changes, in which people attempted to understand their situation, justify their new positions, and control the direction of their common life, varied widely. Some, like the conservative clergy, reaffirmed the value of old structures; others, from Mormons to utopianists, created new kinds of communities and ideologies; still others, like many Jacksonian democrats, celebrated secular individualism and party politics.

In the evangelical world in particular, since the breakdown in 1800 of the informal alliance with Federalism, clergy had been increasingly cut off from their former positions of prestige and power. This exclusion forced them to compete with politicians for moral direction of the nation or else withdraw into a separate sphere of activity. The Beecher-Nettleton system of revivals and moral reform societies at first attempted to preserve the spirit of the old order with a new set of practices and communal structures, but, as we have seen, the waves of revivals rapidly transformed both practice and structure. The Finneyite evangelicals, more nearly in tune with the emerging competitive society, turned increasingly to an ideology of the inner life of the individual as the ultimate unit of the new society. Their emphasis on personal conversion, on intense emotion and individual moral decision over against system and doctrine, was a persuasive strategy. They did not abandon a communal ideal, however. The revivals themselves were emphatically social, and the reform movements which grew out of the revivals represented an attempt to compete with the political order in the shaping of society. The evangelicals' insistence on organizing those of like feeling brought them into conflict with those in the political realm who believed that each individual should form his own opinion, and that any attempt to exert social influence was an infringement of voluntarism and a tyranny over the passions.[2] Under political attack, reinforced by religious conservatives like Colton, the benevolent empire began to crumble. Party politics offered another alternative, and many evangelicals moved toward Whiggery. Others regarded Jacksonian era politics as immoral, and the clergy (who in many places were ineligible for political office) had virtually no options once excluded from political work. Yet withdrawing from the competitive arena would seem to mean giving up the community-of-feeling idea, returning to local churches and denominational boundaries.

Many evangelicals did just that, abandoning reform and large-scale revivals for local church work and a purely pietistic religiosity. Finney himself did not take much interest in the large-scale reform organizations whose leaders he had inspired, and others followed his path, focusing on changing individual hearts, one by one. The years from 1835 to 1857 were marked by localism in religion; the only widespread fervor was the Adventist movement led by William Miller in the early 1840s. Premillenialists did not, however, have much inclination to worry about the larger worldly community. Revivals continued on a seasonal basis in some communities and churches, and there were a few traveling evangelists.[3] Some clergy, while retaining the religious individualism of the Finney style, rejected revivals altogether, thus becoming "liberals." Reform movements generally moved away from their revivalistic roots, sponsoring publications and lectures designed to persuade individuals to petition their congressmen for reform measures. But they were usually cautious about techniques, such as rallies, which would make them vulnerable to accusations that they were stirring up the masses. In short, revivalism and evangelical religion generally became part of a private sphere, a matter of the individual's heart, having little to do with the larger communal structures of the society. It would seem that the fate of the community of feeling was sealed.

Nevertheless, a peculiar combination of circumstances enabled the community-of-feeling ideal to survive. The clergy now presided over an atrophied private realm of their parishioners' hearts. But there they were able to join forces with another group—namely, middle-class women—whose roles too had changed as a result of mobility and industrialization and who were, like the clergy, insulated from the primary processes of government and decision-making. Ann Douglas has described their alliance as it is relevant to the liberal clergy;[4] the case is parallel for the evangelicals. Both appealed to the middle classes, although some evangelicals (especially Methodists and Baptists) tended to speak more to the aspiring middle class than to the solid, well-educated middle-class members of prominent urban Congregational churches.[5] Thanks to the work of Douglas and others such as Barbara Welter and Nancy Cott, it is necessary only to summarize here the character of the cooperation between women and clergy.

Women were defined largely in terms of their roles in the home, as wives and mothers. Nevertheless they had also become, since the early part of the century, the lay backbone of the churches and nonpolitical reform organizations.[6] Women seldom occupied prominent leadership positions in the large organizations, but by midcentury the Methodists were ordaining female clergy, and women had often taken charge of local organizations of the reform societies.[7] Of course, laymen also participated in churches and reform activities, where their financial support was crucial. But for most males, such participation was not the primary definition of their lives. Women and ministers on the contrary had no other lives. They formed an insulated sphere, a community of feeling which the ministers described and the women upheld, but neither had viable means of negotiating for power or exerting direct pressure on government.[8]

Nevertheless women and clergy were able to make a distinctive cultural contribution because they were not toally without resources. Churches were respected and well-supported institutions with active members and financial assets for the support of clergy, moral and religious enterprises outside the church, and publication of periodicals, tracts, and other literature. Women in their role as consumers, whether their income was from husbands, fathers, or their own work outside the home, had money to spend. With less labor necessary at home after industrialization, they often had time and energy to give.[9] In addition, they were increasingly literate and often permitted or encouraged to use their skills in appropriate cultural activities like writing poetry, stories or sketches, novels. It was primarily women and clergy who wrote the lyrics which appear in *Gospel Hymns.* In church and reform activity on the one hand, and in popular literature on the other, women, clergy, and some male writers of women's literature carved out their separate sphere.[10]

In this realm, they developed an ideology of what I will call "evangelical domesticity": of home and woman as primary vehicles of redemptive power, as embodiments of a pure community of feeling. Donald Mitchell, in his popular *Reveries of a Bachelor* (1850), articulated the center of this ideology in his portrait of a happy man who has finally settled down:

> Your dreams of reputation, your swift determination, your impulsive pride, your deep uttered vows to win a name, have all sobered into affection—have all blended into that glow of feeling, which finds its centre, and hope, and joy in HOME. From my soul I pity him whose soul does not leap at the mere utterance of that name.[11]

As Mitchell suggests, a man's home was quite different from his normal world. The realm of woman and family was sharply distinguished from business, politics, and other masculine endeavors. As Walter Houghton has written in *The Victorian Frame of Mind:*

> ... The home [was] a source of virtues which were nowhere else to be found, least of all in business and society. And that in turn made it a place radically different from the surrounding world.... It was a place apart, a walled garden, in which certain virtues too easily crushed by modern life could be preserved, and certain desires of the heart too much thwarted be fulfilled ... a sacred place, a temple.[12]

Despite the separation, the home was also the channel through which women could tame, and ultimately save, the rest of the world. This feature of the ideology made it genuinely evangelical, and it is this which we wish to examine closely, for it is directly relevant to our interpretation of the gospel hymns.

There are innumerable sources to which one could turn to elucidate the ideology of evangelical domesticity. For our purposes, the most compact and readily accessible examples are the evangelical and reform novels which began to appear in the latter half of the nineteenth century. The novel had for a long time remained suspect in many evangelical circles because of its supposed tendency to encourage frivolity and worldliness. Gradually, however, even ministers began to use the form as an instrument of explicitly moral and religious purposes. The result of the acceptance of the form was a rash of religious novels of various types—reform novels, from *Uncle Tom's Cabin* (1852) by Harriet Beecher Stowe to *In His Steps* (1896) by Charles Sheldon, "historical" novels like Lew Wallace's *Ben-Hur* (1880), and didactic novels of heaven like Elizabeth Stuart Phelps's *The Gates Ajar* (1868) and its sequels. To assess their use of domestic images, it will be useful to examine two bestsellers: one a temperance novel, T. S. Arthur's *Ten Nights in a Bar-room, and What I Saw There* (1854); the other a romance, *Barriers Burned Away* by the Reverend E. P. Roe (1872). Although neither is by a woman, the second is by a clergyman. Arthur's book, too, is representative. He was well known as a popular writer for ladies' magazines and an author of tracts on women and family life before *Ten Nights* appeared. Further, as it was devoted to the temperance movement in which large numbers of women participated, it undoubtedly had a wide reading among a female audience.

Most importantly, these two books portray vividly the domestic ideal: home, family, and woman as the sacred center of life in contrast to the masculine world of business and politics with its competition and aggression. The home, as we will see, is a community whose purpose is the ordering of the passions and affections, again in opposition to the external world where emotion and impulse run wild.[13] Home and woman become the source of salvation and/or reform precisely because of their capacity to provide order and stability in that way. The two novels will enable us to observe the continuity of such themes over a span of time as well as some of the important elaborations on the strategy of evangelical domesticity—which was, in effect, the latest incarnation of the "community of feeling."

Although Timothy Shay Arthur was himself a Swedenborgian, his works were already a staple of evangelical literature when he published *Ten Nights in a Bar-room* in 1854.[14] The book quickly became a bestseller and was a favorite of the temperance movement for years. It is written from the viewpoint of a businessman who during the course of his travels has occasion to stop in the town of Cedarville, staying one or more nights at a time, for a total of ten nights (spanning a period of eight years). He lodges each time at the "Sickle and Sheaf," a tavern new at the opening of the book, owned by a man named Simon Slade. The book describes in lurid detail the degeneration of the tavern, the town, and its inhabitants, to make the argument for legal prohibition of the liquor traffic.

The opening scenes show a proud and happy Simon Slade, former miller now turned tavern-keeper, with two pleasant teenage children and a good wife (although Mrs. Slade is already ill at ease with her husband's new profession). The tavern is doing a bustling business among the town's best gentlemen and most promising youth. There are only two dark spots in the circle of happy family and friends: one, a "poor, broken-down inebriate," Joe Morgan, a former partner of Slade's at the mill; and the other, the archvillain of the melodrama, Harvey Green, a mysterious character with no known roots and no obvious source of income. We are told immediately that "unscrupulous selfishness was written all over his sinister countenance" and that he was "a man of evil passions"; soon we learn that he is by trade a gambler.[15] It is no surprise that Green figures in the first incident which adumbrates the novel's structure of the disruption of the happy-family image by events resulting from the effects of alcohol.

This first disruption takes the form of an argument between Green and a minor character named Lyon; its description sets a pattern for later incidents:

> Green had scarcely finished the sentence, ere he was lying at full length upon the floor! The other had sprung upon him like a tiger, and with one blow from his heavy fist, struck him down as if he had been a child. For a moment or two, Green lay stunned and bewildered—then, starting up with a savage cry, that sounded more bestial than human, he drew a long knife from a concealed sheath, and attempted to stab his assailant; but the murderous purpose was not accomplished, for the other man, who had superior strength and coolness, saw the

> design, and with a well-directed blow almost broke the arm of Green, causing the knife to leave his hand and glide far across the room.
>
> "I'm half tempted to wring your neck off," exclaimed the man, whose name was Lyon, now much excited; and seizing Green by the throat, he strangled him until his face grew black. . . .
>
> Judge Lyman and the landlord now interfered, and rescued Green from the hands of his fully aroused antagonist. For some time they stood growling at each other, like two parted dogs, struggling to get free, in order to renew the conflict, but gradually cooled off. (p. 26)

The scene is instructive not only for its portrayal of the violent emotions released by drink, but also in its imagery—the men are tigers, beasts, dogs. The reduction of men to less-than-human creatures consumed by animal passions, goes on beneath the jovial surface of the inn's atmosphere.

On the second "night," one year later, the same theme is taken up again. Passion has laid its ugly hand already on those who frequent the tavern. Simon Slade's son, Frank, for example, described in Chapter 1 of the book in terms of his "deep blue eyes, from which innocence beamed" and the "girl-like beauty of his face," now had a rounder face with a "gross, sensual expression." Harvey Green of course is laughing with a chilling, inhuman cackle, while the whole conversation of the tavern has degenerated into profanity, vulgarity, and obscenity. The explosion occurs soon after Joe Morgan's little girl, who comes to the inn every night looking for her drunken father, enters the tavern to plead with him to come home. Slade is in a rage at Morgan for some unspecified cause, and in a fit of anger throws an empty glass at him. He misses his aim and the glass strikes Mary instead, wounding her—fatally, as it turns out. Demon rum has caused not only the pitiful scene of a little girl wandering out at night in search of her father, but now also a direct attack on her as an exemplar of purity.[16]

A further example of the problems associated with liquor appears when the narrator takes us to the Morgan household. Before Mary dies, she persuades her father to promise he will never drink again. His attempt to abstain, however, carries him into the throes of "drunkard's madness": his nerves shattered by the use of "unnatural stimulants," he hallucinates toads, black cats, and other frightful creatures in every corner. He is calmed by the ministrations of his wife and the gentle influence of Mary, his "good angel," and finally achieves the power to keep his vow. Nonetheless the scene demonstrates another and equally bestial side of the coin of intemperance, according to Arthur's ideology: not only anger and violence, as with Green and Slade, but also derangement—both perversions of the true and honorable human affections.

As time passes, the world of the "Sickle and Sheaf" grows more and more ragged at the edges, the decline more obvious. Five years later the narrator finds the place filthy, its inhabitants lazy, and an Irish bartender and waitresses having taken the places of Mr. and Mrs. Slade as host and hostess—in all, a total eradication of the "homey" image of bygone years. Green has remained the same, cold and sinister, but one young man after another has been drawn into his "vortex of ruin." When the youths are not gambling and drinking, they are off gunning, fishing, and racing horses. But perhaps the most striking personal description is that of Judge Lyman, a local politician:

> Five years had marred that face terribly. It seemed twice the former size; and all its bright expression was gone.

> The thickened and protruding eyelids half closed the leaden eyes, and the swollen lips and cheeks gave to his countenance a look of all-predominating sensuality. True manliness had bowed itself in debasing submission to the bestial. He talked loudly, and with a pompous dogmatism—mainly on political subjects—but talked only from memory; for any one could see, that thought came into but feeble activity. And yet, derationalized, so to speak, as he was, through drink, he had been chosen a representative in Congress, at the previous election, on the anti-temperance ticket, and by a very handsome majority. (p. 126)

All the characters (except for Joe Morgan, now on his way up again) have become more beastly, inhuman, violent. Even the women who never enter the bar have been affected: Mrs. Slade is worn and haggard, while the mother of Willy Hammond, formerly one of the most promising young men of the town, wanders the streets looking for the boy she idolized, her reason nearly gone from her suffering. We witness a series of violent events: there is another argument, Harvey Green murders Willy Hammond, a mob lynches Green, and the whole tavern turns into a brawling mass, complete with eyes gouged out and bloody wounds, in front of Green's coffin. Finally, two years later, the culmination comes when Frank Slade, now also fully deteriorated into sensuality, kills his father in a petty argument. That final horror induces the citizens of Cedarville to stop the town's liquor traffic.

The course of the novel is a reiteration, intricately worked out, of the idea that the curse of liquor is its perversion of home and family, women and children, through the distortion of the affections. The killings point to the destruction of domesticity: Slade kills innocent Mary Morgan, the perfect child; Green slays Willy Hammond, the perfect son of a doting mother; and finally there is parricide, Frank killing Simon Slade. Further, Arthur employs a twist of setting from the ordinary domestic novel to make the horrors all the more obvious. The tavern is supposed to be the Slades' home and also a "home away from home" for travelers, but Simon Slade turns it into an instrument of his own lust for money, and thereby makes it the scene of antidomestic events, from the deals of politicians like Lyman to Green's gambling den in his room. Meanwhile, the women and children who are supposed to be at home are outside, frantically roaming the dark streets, searching for their errant men.

The inversion of place parallels the distortion of the affections which, as we have seen, takes the form of violence, bestiality, and insanity. Liquor's evil "influences" on the passions are really the heart of the matter; that is shown clearly in Arthur's summary of the decline of Frank Slade. He had been his mother's "worshipped boy"; but, Arthur tells us,

> from the day the tavern opened, and Frank drew into his lungs full draughts of the changed atmosphere by which he was now surrounded, the work of moral deterioration commenced. The very smell of the liquor exhilarated him unnaturally; while the subjects of conversation, so new to him, that found discussion in the bar-room, soon came to occupy a prominent place in his imagination, to the exclusion of those humane, childlike, tender, and heavenly thoughts and impressions it had been the mother's care to impart and awaken.
>
> Ah! with what an eager zest does the heart drink in of evil. And how almost hopeless is the case of a boy, surrounded, as Frank was, by the corrupting, debasing associations of a bar-room! Had his father meditated his ruin, he could not have more surely laid his plans for the fearful consummation; and he reaped as he had sown. With a selfish desire to get gain, he embarked in the trade of

> corruption, ruin, and death, weakly believing that he and his could pass through the fire harmless. (p. 209)

Liquor had transformed the very "atmosphere"; Frank's "imagination" had been corrupted and debased by the "unnatural exhilaration" of it; and thus he had become inhuman. The truly human is in fact the childlike or the motherly: "those humane, childlike, tender, and heavenly thoughts" his mother had tried to teach him. His father's lust for profit had, in Beecher's metaphor, opened the cave of Aeolus and brought the winds of passion to attack humanity from every direction. Arthur does not hesitate to use related metaphors himself, metaphors which are familiar to us from the gospel hymns. He describes Willy Hammond early in the novel as teetering on the "brink of a fearful precipice. . . . The clouds were gathering already, and the low rumble of the distant thunder presaged the coming of a fearful tempest" (pp. 33–34); and he speaks of the town's young men drawn into "the whirling circles that narrow toward a vortex of ruin" (p. 137). The world of chaos, of storms and whirlpools, of violent and bestial passions, threaten the tender, feminine and childlike, domestic affections.

In the battle of home and tavern, the female world versus the male one, domestic affections over against lustful passions, the world is winning. The only solution is to control the world by the instrument of law. That, at any rate, is the lesson promulgated by Arthur, writing at the height of the temperance crusade of the early 1850s. Yet his work also displays another way. The one character who is truly saved, Joe Morgan, comes back to his senses and to an orderly life through another means—a domestic miracle, so to speak—the loving, sacrificial death of his angel child. The event is significant for understanding the evangelical ideology, even though Arthur does not highlight it (since it would not be particularly helpful to his argument for legal prohibition) and even though it seems a mere convention. Precisely because it is a convention, however, it reveals something important about the popular ideology: the domestic circle of love and affection not only is under attack, but also is the principal mainstay against the encroachments of the world upon the affections. It is useful to recall a similar two-sidedness in Beecher's plea for protection of women: on the one hand, their delicate sensibilities should be protected from the corruption which comes from praying or performing in public; on the other, they are important in having a "soothing, civilizing influence on man"—they are the source of sensibilities and civilization. That in turn makes their protection all the more important. Arthur expresses the same ambivalence: we must protect our women and children from the damage that liquor can do; yet they are the chief hope in saving us from the damage that liquor has done.

Such a use of the domestic conventions is not unique to *Ten Nights*. As John William Ward has observed, Harriet Beecher Stowe's *Uncle Tom's Cabin* takes much the same perspective. Her presentation of the problem of the novel is "a world threatened by instability, a world of individuals seeking a resting place, seeking no less than a home," while "the tragedy of the Negro is that he has, quite literally, no home."[17] Slavery had destroyed home and family, tearing people from one another, and it was threatening the world of white men as well. The only solution to the problem, as Stowe herself said, was to "*feel right,*"[18] and those who know how to "feel right" in the novel are women, children, and Negroes,[19] namely the "domestics." There, as in *Ten Nights,* domesticity and the realm of the affections hang precariously in the midst of a chaotic world, while simultaneously they provide a counterbalance to the threat of chaos in the institutions of society, offering the possibility of emotional and social peace and order. This had become standard popular ideology by the middle of the nineteenth century. The special, even redemptive, role of home and women in such novels was, however, to reach an even higher level in succeeding bestsellers.

Edward Payson Roe's novel, *Barriers Burned Away,*[20] opens with a scene of a pale, shawled woman seated at the window of a weather-beaten house on the prairie, gazing anxiously across the snow. One half expects, after the horrors of *Ten Nights,* to discover that she is waiting fearfully for a drunken husband to return home. But fortunately that is not the case. Rather, Ethel Fleet is watching for her son Dennis, who has been called home from college to be at his father's deathbed; and, happily, he soon arrives. The deathbed scene then takes place, focusing more on the figure of the mother than on the dying man.

Dennis's father has spent his life in pursuit of one money-making scheme or another, each ending in failure. He has no faith left in God, and is barely prevented by Dennis and Ethel from ending his life with a curse to God on his lips. Then, as he sleeps during his last night on earth, his wife prays for him. She is a woman of perfect faith, virtually living in heaven even while on earth:

> When alone, in moments of rest from incessant toil, she would take down the great family Bible, and with her finger on some description of the "new heavens and new earth," . . . she would look away with that intent gaze. The new world, purged from sin and sorrow, would rise before her with more than Edenlike loveliness. Her spirit would revel in its shadowy walks and sunny glades, and as

> the crowning joy she would meet her Lord and Saviour in some secluded place, and sit listening at his feet like Mary of old. (p. 9)

Her intense spirituality shows its power almost immediately, as her prayers for her husband are answered. He tells her of his experience:

> ". . . I commenced calling out in my heart, 'God be merciful to me—a sinner. Then while I prayed, I seemed to see my Saviour's face right above your bowed head. Oh, how reproachfully He looked at me! and yet his expression was full of love, too. . . . Then it seemed that I fell down at His feet and wept bitterly, and as I did so the look of reproach passed away, and only an expression of love and forgiveness remained. A sudden peace came into my soul. . . . Ethel, dear, my patient, much enduring wife, I believe God has answered your prayer. I feel that I am a new man." (pp. 12–13)

The faithful, praying woman who walks "in the garden" (as the hymns would have it) with Jesus, and is all but identified with Jesus himself; the focus of concern on the circle of close relationships; the power of prayer—all those remain themes throughout the novel. They find expression primarily in the figure of Ethel's son Dennis, who is the hero of the story.

After his father's death, Dennis must go out into the world to make a living in order to support his mother and younger sisters. The remainder of the book relates his trials in the great city of Chicago: how he starts at the bottom, much to his dismay, but gradually proves his "gentlemanly" character and native abilities, builds a foundation for future success, and wins the woman he loves. In the way Dennis's battles are articulated and in descriptions of his triumph, the images of passion and domesticity come to the fore, now applied to new objects.

His first enemy is the city itself and its potential evil influences. He finds people unfriendly, shrewd, and narrow-minded. Trying to find his way back to his rooming house—which is, unbeknownst to him, the most disreputable place in Chicago—he gets lost. He faces the temptation of liquor, first directly and then indirectly, when he is offered a job as a bartender, but overcomes those. Finally, when he moves out of his room, the proprietor cheats him out of some money. The harshness of the city and the sequence of unpleasant events have raised his emotions to the boiling point, and this last incident tempts him to fight the man. He barely succeeds in conquering his anger by remembering—of course—his mother. Roe writes: "There is a latent tiger in every man. But a hand seemed to hold him back, and a sober second thought came over him. What! Dennis Fleet, the son of Ethel Fleet, brawling, fighting in a bar-room, a gambling den . . . !" (p. 35). The scene shows that mothers' influences had grown stronger since the time of *Ten Nights,* so happily Dennis escapes the first series of snares which await every young man in the city. He even becomes speculative about it later: "Perhaps very many come to the city in the morning of life like this snow, pure and unstained; but after being here awhile they become like this snow when it has been tossed about and trodden under every careless foot" (p. 54). The child is pure but polluted by the worldliness of the city; only the mother's influence can save him.

The city itself is a source of danger, but it is not to be Dennis's chief problem. There are two other victories yet to win. First he becomes involved in helping the Bruders, a German immigrant family. Mr. Bruder was once a fine artist, but his appetite for drink has become a disease and, as might be expected, has led the family down the path to ruin. Dennis learns of their troubles through one of the Bruder children who is in his Sunday-school class. As soon as he earns a little money, he pays a visit to the family; and just in time, for the father is about to sell his last remaining painting, spend the money on a final binge, and then kill himself. We find the same sorts of descriptions as in *Ten Nights:* Mr. Bruder has "bloodshot eyes," a "purple, bloated face," and is subject to "violent impulses" and "mad frenzies"; his wife has put up a heroic struggle but it has made her "prematurely old, broken in health, broken in heart"; the children are "half-famished young animals," devouring crusts under the table like "hungry little wolves." There is a touch of foreignness here beyond the bestial and irrational, however, because Roe writes the characters' dialogue in a thick German accent ("Mine Gott be praised!" "I vill do vatever you vant me to") and emphasizes their poverty as making a difference in their status—although Dennis nobly ignores that and indeed overcomes it.

By Dennis's good will and financial aid (he pays Bruder for giving him art lessons) their forlorn condition is soon corrected. Just from being treated like a "gentleman," Bruder's attitude changes immediately:

> Old associations and feelings, seemingly long dead, awoke. . . . Then his artist-nature began to quicken into life again. . . . Something like hope and exultation began to light up his sullen, heavy features; thought and feeling began to spiritualize and ennoble what but a little before had been so coarse and repulsive. (p. 119)

The instantaneous transformation of the bestial passions into spiritual affections is hedged about with the qualification that Bruder has a great struggle before him, but the outcome is never really in doubt. Dennis, acting consciously in imitation of Christ, has uplifted the man's feelings, and through him the whole family, by becoming their friend. Subsequently, the household becomes a second family to him. When he falls sick, Bruder goes home with him to help nurse him; at the end of the novel, Dennis takes the children in a temporary emergency.

The battle that engages most of Dennis's energies is, however, not the Bruders but another German family, the Ludolphs. Dennis acquires employment as porter and man-of-all-work at the Art Building, owned by Mr. Ludolph, and then gradually proves his worth and moves up to the position of head salesman. In the meantime, he also falls in love with Ludolph's daughter, the beautiful society girl Christine. The problem is precisely the reverse of the Bruders' situation in terms of differences in status. Mr. Ludolph is of noble blood, son of a German baron, but not well off financially due to adverse circumstances in his homeland. He had come to the United States to make enough money in the art business to return to Germany and marry Christine to a nobleman. Ludolph is, Roe tells us, "Napoleonic" in his ambition, greed, selfishness, and shrewdness, a "thrifty Teuton" and also an infidel. He has some artistic taste but imposes a cool order in the store which his German clerks (who speak with the telltale accent, unlike Ludolph and his daughter) carry to the extreme. Dennis's own natural talent for artistic arrangement is the principal reason for his rapid promotion over them.

Ludolph has raised his daughter to accord with his personal ambitions—to make her proud, aspiring to nobility, selfish, and cold. She has become skeptical of religion and even of love and romance ("which," Roe notes, "in many young hearts is religion's shadow"). Hers is a "cold, negative" life in contrast to Dennis's "earnest and positive" one. The problem is how to warm the icy heart of Christine, not merely that Dennis might win her love (although his struggle between such a selfish motive and higher ones is a theme of the novel) but also as a fundamentally religious problem. Dennis expresses his hopes by painting two symbolic pictures: one of Christine asleep in an ice-filled grotto from which Dennis is trying to awaken her; the other of him leading her out of the cave into a spring landscape.

> The icy hue and rigidity were all gone. She stood in the warm sunlight, and seemed all warmth and life. Her face glowed with feeling, yet was full of peace. . . .
>
> Everything, in contrast with the frozen, deathlike cave, indicated life, activity. Near her, a plane-tree, which in nature's language is the emblem of genius, towered into the sky; around its trunk twined the passion-flower, meaning, in Flora's tongue, "Holy love"; while just above her head, sipping the nectar from an open blossom, was a bright-hued butterfly, the symbol of immortality. By her side stood the same tall, manly form, with face still averted. He was pointing and her eyes, softened, and yet lustrous and happy, were following where a path wound through a long vista, in alternate light and shadow, to a gate, that in the distance looked like a pearl. Above and beyond it, in airy outline, rose the walls and towers of the Holy City, the New Jerusalem. (pp. 293–94)

The resolution would have to come, the painting suggests, through not only the "natural" course of love and marriage but also conversion.

The path to such an ending is of course fraught with difficulties. The Ludolphs regard Dennis as far beneath them on the chain of being—Christine twice compares him to her greyhound, Wolf. Even as she begins to appreciate the finer elements of his character, she tries to use them only to satisfy her artistic ambitions, ultimately enticing Dennis into a declaration of love so that she can paint his face to capture the feelings she cannot feel herself. His discovery of her deception throws him into a prolonged illness. He returns home, where his mother and Mr. Bruder nurse him back to health and, significantly, to a greater spirituality in his attitude toward Christine and toward life in general. From then on, he is as strong as his mother, yet still tender toward Christine; and Roe compares him more and more frequently to the "Divine Friend" who "waits and watches" over her. She, meanwhile, is trying to forget him but agonizes deeply over what she did to him.

The denouement comes in the great Chicago fire of October 1871. Dennis saves Christine from the flames, but all her possessions are burned, and her father dies a gruesome death while trying to rescue valuable papers from the Art Building. Nevertheless, thanks to the prayers of Dennis, his mother, and finally her own, Christine is converted on the beach at Lake Michigan: "Turning to the still raging flames, she exclaimed, 'Burn on with your fiery billows, I do not fear you now! I am safe, safe forever!' " (p. 426). Shortly thereafter, they end up at a church with a motley crew of refugees, including a former drunkard whom Dennis had met during his first days in Chicago, and the Bruder children, and they have a family-style dinner with a toast to "the United States of Ameriky." Then, before the ashes of Christine's former home, she and Dennis pledge their love to one another.

That romantic conclusion is, much more directly than in *Ten Nights,* the consequence of an evangelical domesticity—the home circle being equated with the highest spiritual life, the path to conversion, the earthly counterpart of heaven. Most obviously that is expressed through Dennis's mother, an image of perfection similar to Mary Morgan in Arthur's novel. The ties of Ethel Fleet with her son are emphasized throughout, with letters or direct contact between them at crucial points. It is only after she has nursed him through the crisis of illness that she calmly departs for heaven, leaving Dennis strong enough to manage things on his own. Even then, she is part of the strength of his faith; as he tells Christine during the fire, he is not afraid because "Heaven and mother are just beyond this tempest." The tie of love between man and woman is nearly as strong, however, since romance is "religion's shadow." As Mrs. Fleet informs Dennis, marriage is "the emblem of the spiritual oneness of the believer's soul with Christ"; and, as one of Christine's friends tells her, what she needed was "love to God and some good man." Finally, of course, there are the domestic ties—of adoption, so to speak—created by "friendly" action, as in Dennis's being brother to the Bruders.

The domestic circle does more than simply perpetuate itself, however. It is not merely the locus of love between intimates; nor is it, as in *Ten Nights,* a possible solution to one social problem, although certainly Dennis faces and conquers liquor for himself and for Mr. Bruder. The sphere of home and family extends wider than that, involving matters of socioeconomic class, political ideology, and national identity. Dennis Fleet raises the Bruders from poverty and brings Christine down from high society. Simultaneously, he proves the worth of democracy over autocratic notions—or rather, that is proved by the fire, which destroys all basis for aristocratic pretense and, as Roe repeatedly tells us, levels all distinctions. Further, by using German immigrants for the two extremes, Roe makes Dennis show the superiority of Yankee warmth, practicality, and self-control over Europe's heated passions, on the one hand, and its icy coldness and rigidity on the other. The conversion of Christine at the end is to democratic, middle-class American experience as well as to home and Jesus.

All those distinctions, however, are still portrayed as matters of the passions or affections. The problem with Bruder is that his passions have gotten out of control, while Christine has no feeling at all. Roe's adoption of a popular ideology about art, too, makes it possible for him to emphasize sublime feeling as the center of the Christian experience. And finally, he makes generous use of the metaphors of nature to present the world as a mass of chaotic passions—as we have learned to expect. Dennis, before his illness, was "like a ship that had been driven hither and thither, tempest-tossed and in danger. At last, under a clear sky and in smooth water, it finds its true bearings, and steadily pursues the homeward voyage." Christine when under conviction is "tossed on a sea of uncertainty and fear, . . . in darkness and weakness." "I seem," she says, "on a narrow island, the ocean is all around me, and the tide is rising, *rising*." The Chicago fire is of course the culmination of all this heavy-handed symbolism, and we have already seen how Christine addressed the "fiery billows" there. It might be noted further that in the midst of it all, when crowds have waded out into the lake to escape the flames, Dennis rallies the Christians around him by singing a hymn—Charles Wesley's "Jesus, Lover of My Soul"—a religious act which creates a safe space in the midst of chaos.[21]

For Roe, social problems could be encompassed by viewing them as aspects of a religious problem which in turn could be solved by bringing people to the right "temperature" (to return to Finney's metaphor for feeling) and by making them all part of one happy family which dissolves their differences. That theme too would be taken up again, two decades later, by Charles Sheldon in his famous *In His Steps*. Sheldon deals much more explicitly and thoroughly with class distinctions and the mediating position of the American middle class, as Wayne

Elzey has shown in a stimulating essay.[22] The novel asks the question, "What would Jesus do?"—what would he do about the poor masses in the cities? A sermon on the subject "warms up" the well-to-do enough that they begin to work toward society's improvement. The real difficulties, however, stem from having to "cool down" the poor, who are seen not as individuals, as in Roe's novel, but as a besotted mass called "the Rectangle" (the name for the slum section of town). All the language of evil passions, turmoil, and heat is transferred onto them in Sheldon's portrayal. The solution is nevertheless the same, finally a domestic one: revivals led by the beautiful singing of a compassionate woman, and the founding of a settlement house in the heart of the city, where people can come for solace and where girls can be taught to cook and clean.[23] Salvation is not far from home.

In such novels, the nineteenth-century images of home and family, of woman and the tender affections, are employed in a variety of ways. In *Ten Nights,* Arthur appeals to the notion of home and family as especially vulnerable and pleads for its protection from the onslaughts of evil. Yet he also, through the Morgan family, reveals the potential redemptive power of the home circle and domestic figures. Roe in *Barriers Burned Away* emphasizes that power still more, while painting a complex portrait of society in which home and woman become the primary mediating and tempering influence. If there are any barriers to be overcome, any extremes of passion to be softened, we can have recourse to the complex of intimate affections represented by mother, lover, and friend—figures explicitly Christ-like in their feelings and actions. Roe's novel shows the domestic circle involved in the affairs of the world, yet always—and this is common to both books—fundamentally opposed to it: a haven of spirituality and deep feeling, an enclave of safety and power in a hostile and chaotic world.

The development of the ideology of domesticity in that direction made it an excellent strategy for solving the problem of order and passion by, as it were, putting passion in its place. It provided a useful set of images and metaphors which evangelicals could appropriate for their purposes. When revivals returned to nationwide prominence in 1857, they were already emphasizing the family and especially maternal ties, as we will see in the next chapter. By the time of Moody and Sankey, the language of evangelical domesticity had thoroughly infused the forms of the revival, and those evangelists took it still further. Such developments in rhetoric were possible and persuasive because of the clarification which the domestic image provided for the problem of the passions and for understanding the relation of Christians to the rest of the world. We saw in Chapter 3 that Finney and his fellow revivalists had invented a dualistic understanding of the world—Christians versus non-Christians, according to their *feelings*—but they ran into difficulties when they were accused of setting themselves up as tyrants over other people's feelings. The domestic image provided the necessary conceptual tools for making the proper distinctions. One might say, adapting a phrase from Claude Lévi-Strauss, that within this system emotions were not only good to feel but good to think.[24] The image of wife and mother in the home, the gentle feminine influence over against evil and degenerate men of the world, showed forth vividly the contrast between good and evil passion. The home contained emotions in a sacred sphere, sobering them into a "glow of feeling," as in the quotation from Donald Mitchell earlier in this chapter. From this viewpoint, religion could no longer be criticized for stirring up wild passions, as had happened in the Finney era. Nor could the community of feeling—the domestic circle—be portrayed as a dictatorial organization. Emotions were carefully controlled and purified within the home. The source of evil was external—liquor, politics, profit-seeking, urban life. All these caused the degeneration of the mind into bestiality, irrationality, aggressiveness, or (as in Roe's Mr. Ludolph) cold calculation.

The contrasts between home and world became, in the hands of writers like Roe, the basis on which one could also understand religious assertions about Jesus and heaven. Roe, Stowe, and others employed a parallelism between the domestic ideology and a popular theology, which appears also in the gospel hymns. The most direct way of explicating this parallelism is to schematize the dualistic system that Arthur and Roe employ. The following sets of contrasts are among the most important in their stories:

Negative versus	Positive
Worldliness, men, money, politics, liquor (Simon Slade, Judge Lyman; Mr. Ludolph)	Home, mothers, children (Mary Morgan; Ethel and Dennis Fleet)
Lust, violence, insanity, bestiality; fear, sorrow	Tenderness, love, nurture
Tempest, fires, wandering	Calm, rest, safety
Temptation and dissipation (i.e., real weakness)	Strength in apparent weakness
This world	Jesus and heaven

Each of the characteristics on the left appears in description and metaphor as associated with worldly, antidomestic, chaotic, and disorderly forces and people; those on the right are central to the ideal home-family-mother complex. Characters in the novels move between the two. Frank Slade begins on the right as a lovely, girlish child, then moves to the left as liquor weakens him, producing violence and insanity. Joe Morgan begins on the left, but thanks to his daughter Mary he moves right; so does Christine Ludolph, through the intervention of Dennis and Ethel Fleet acting as Friend and Mother. This is, of course, equivalent to conversion—always through the agency of a Christ-like character from the right-hand side. Other uses of the dualism are possible, as when Roe associates domesticity with the middle classes versus higher and lower classes and with Yankee virtues versus European ones. Similarly, Harriet Beecher Stowe works her own variations using black slaves as exemplars of evangelical domesticity; and it would be instructive to analyze *Uncle Tom's Cabin* in these terms to elucidate Stowe's views of the South, New England, and the Midwest. But that is only to suggest how pervasive the system is. It represents a strategy for defining the world in terms of a coherent and vivid set of metaphors and images.

The similarity between this set of contrasts and that of the gospel-hymn metaphors discussed in Chapter 2 is quite striking. The most important, we may recall, were the following: negative versus positive emotions, turmoil versus rest, and weakness versus strength. These are precisely parallel to the novels' primary themes and metaphors: love versus fear and insanity, safety versus storms and wanderings, strength versus temptation. In both, the passions are the problem, and passivity is the solution. The specific articulations of these are not always precisely the same. For example, the hymns do not present negative emotions in terms of violence and bestiality; they speak instead of inner struggles, "fightings within and fears without," as in "Just As I Am." Yet that does not contradict the novels. Women in the novels are those who undergo sorrow and inner struggle, while those who become violent beasts are men, exposed to the chaotic forces of the outside world. Further, such forces are depicted in similar ways in both hymns and novels, as storms and turbulent ocean waves. The hymn lyrics have, so to speak, abstracted such metaphors from other context where they are clearly related not only to natural forces as in Roe's novel, but also to social ones, as when Arthur calls up an image of a whirlpool to describe the young men sucked into Harvey Green's "vortex of ruin." On the positive side, Roe's portrait of Ethel Fleet conversing with Jesus in sunny glades seems designed to parallel hymns like "In the Secret of His Presence." In short, the hymns incorporate the ordering of the world provided by the ideology of evangelical domesticity in the novels: the two rhetorics are parallel and very nearly identical. Jesus and heaven, so central in the hymns, are being understood in terms of domestic descriptions. The tender affections, the feminine virtues, the home/haven which gives protection and generates inward strength through intimacy—all become part of the hymns' picture of Jesus and his heavenly realm.

Yet at this point it may seem that we are making too great a leap from novels to hymns. The evangelical novel may have appealed to a more elite audience than did *Gospel Hymns.* Certainly it appeared in a different setting, in the parlor or drawing room, whereas the hymns were part of a communal activity. The novel can serve us, as we saw earlier, only as the most easily accessible source for explicating the ideology. But it is possible to show more specifically the relation of evangelical domesticity to the hymns as part of a larger community of feeling by examining the revivalistic practice which prevailed after 1850.

5

The Taming of the Spirit: The New Urban Revivals

THE rhetoric of evangelical domesticity came to the fore in mass revivals whose setting differed considerably from those of the 1820s and 1830s. As we saw at the beginning of Chapter 4, the antirevivalist rhetoric had led to a retreat of revivalism from the public sphere and a change in the reform movements born of the revivals. The impulse behind the antislavery and temperance movements had been channeled into petitions to legislatures or party (especially third-party) platforms, the reforms thus becoming political rather than religious issues during the 1840s. The temperance people had achieved a political victory with the passage of the Maine Law in 1851, but their triumph was only temporary. The remaining benevolent societies, such as the Bible and tract societies and the American Sunday-School Union, kept themselves apart from any activity which might be construed as political. Even when the Sunday-school movement experienced a resurgence of activism after the Civil War, in the hands of men like Dwight L. Moody, writer and editor Edward Eggleston, and businessmen John Wanamaker and H. J. Heinz, its purposes were solely devotional and educational: the promotion of "social Christianity" and evangelism.[1] The most important new organization in the late 1850s, the Young Men's Christian Association, was activist in seeking conversions and moral reform but had explicitly adopted the domestic ideal as its model, committing itself to providing a "home away from home" for young men in the cities. The original Boston constitution of the organization stated its intent of being

> a social organization of those in whom the love of Christ has produced love to men; who shall meet the young stranger as he enters our city, take him by the hand, direct him to a boarding house where he may find a quiet home pervaded with Christian influences, introduce him to the Church and Sabbath School, bring him to the Rooms of the Association and in every way throw around him good influences, so that he may feel that he is not a stranger, but that noble and Christian spirits care for his soul.. . .[2]

The emphasis on "influences" and the model of the "quiet home" reveals the nature of this *social* organization. In the YMCA as in other organizations, the evangelicals had learned well the lessons of the Finney era: activism had to be limited to strictly social and religious purposes, outside of the political arena.

The mark of those lessons had been imprinted on the revivals themselves, especially in terms of avoidance of overemotionality. When nationwide revivals occurred in 1857–58 and 1875–77 with Moody and Sankey,[3] observers and defenders insisted that they were totally under control: there was no "undue excitement," the meetings were pervaded by "deep solemnity." Proponents of the 1857–58 revival were proud of the lack "of machinery or of human instrumentality to work upon the feelings."[4] Similarly, an observer of Moody's revivals proclaimed rhapsodically that "the Spirit is among us, not so much as the rushing, mighty wind, bearing down with violence all obstacles: nor even so much, perhaps, as the 'floods upon the dry ground,' but rather as the gentle summer rain, or the silently falling dew.. . ."[5] Not that feeling and emotion were no longer important—they were indeed, but they were tame and gentle compared to the agonies and ecstasies of the Finney era. The continuity between the two periods appears in the recurring emphasis on "sympathy," the "contagion" of earnestness, the "blending together" of participants, the "bond of union" created by prayer.[6] "Feeling," wrote one chronicler in a tender vein, "is the warmth that thaws the frosty intellect so that the seed can drop into it, and then nurses that germ into growth. Feeling is the wind in the sails of intellect that blows it on to a grand voyage."[7] Still too, people thought of "influence" as a kind of atmosphere or intangible power comparable to steam or electricity. They were especially fascinated with the telegraph as an instrument of God to spread the 1857–58 revival.[8] The ideology of the community of feeling had survived from the revivals of the 1830s, but the more violent uses of emotion had virtually disappeared.[9]

Paralleling the continuity in the revivalists' notions of feeling, the forms of social religion remained from the earlier era. Indeed, prayer, testimony, and hymn became even more prominent, ousting the sermon in the 1857–58 "lay revival." This revival was built upon prayer and testimony, precisely orchestrated and controlled, within the framework of lunch-hour meetings for the benefit of businessmen.[10] Launched in October 1857 by one Jeremiah Lamphier, a lay missionary at the William Street Dutch Reformed Church in New York City, the idea soon spread to other churches and other cities, until nearly every major urban area in the North had large daily meetings going on in the churches in their business centers. The prayer meetings followed roughly the same form: hymn, brief Scripture reading, prayer by the leader; prayer and exhortation by those in attendance; silent prayer at the halfway point of the meeting; then more prayer, testimony, and singing.[11] The larger meetings often received requests for prayer and reports of answered prayer from others unable to attend. In some places too, the prayer meeting was followed by a meeting for inquiry, at which individuals could converse with experienced Christians.[12]

Although the Moody-Sankey revivals of the 1870s featured the two evangelists as "stars," and their mass public meetings drew the largest crowds, their revival tours were still built upon the structure of prayer and inquiry meetings. Local church personnel prepared for the visits of Moody and Sankey through a series of advance prayer meetings. During the four- to six-week crusades, noon prayer meetings occurred every weekday, and inquiry meetings after each evening mass meeting. In addition, there were special meetings for various classes of people—women, young men, soldiers, workingmen, college students, children—and meetings on the temperance cause and on Bible study.[13] Prayer, testimony, and exhortation, the basic forms of social religion, were the foundation of all those gatherings.

The purposes of such forms of worship had not changed much since the earlier revivals. Prayer and testimony were vehicles for the articulation of emotion, individually and socially, as well as for the worship of God. Participants showed little interest in intense emotionalism for its own sake, however, as in the agonizing prayer of the early Finney revivals. The aim instead was a happy medium of controlled affection, shared by a community and directed to God. Prayer first of all helped the individual achieve a proper mental state. One businessman, commenting on the 1857–58 prayer meetings, was quoted as saying, "If I could not get some half hours every day to pray myself into a right state of mind, I should certainly be overburdened and disheartened, or do such things as no Christian man ought," namely, either "break down or turn rascal."[14] Second, prayer was to create a channel of communication between people and God. Henry C. Fish wrote in his 1874 revival handbook that prayer "enters into the plan and structure of the universe. The remark of some one is not too strong, that God would as soon give the rain without the clouds or the electric fluid, as revivals without the prayers of his people."[15] Prayer was a power comparable to natural forces which, generated from among the people at social meetings, achieved "influence" with God.

Commentators equally recognized the importance of testimony—the "news of others' conversion," as Fish quoted Jonathan Edwards.[16] Even Moody, who generally did not emphasize the practice of relating "experience," nevertheless admitted that conversion is "sometimes best done by believers giving an account of the joy they experience in believing, instead of exhorting."[17] Charles L. Thompson, discussing in 1877 the revivals of his own time, emphasized the importance of interchange between people during inquiry meetings on the grounds that it was congruent with the constitution of the human mind and the nature of the gospel itself: Jesus had personally sought and saved, more than preached. "Moral influence," he wrote,

> is at its highest when it moves from one heart to another. . . . God has adjusted every moral force in the universe for the purpose of accelerating the progress of truth. Chief among these moral forces are those which lie

> in the line of the human and natural affections. The gospel gets an impulse in passing through a human heart which it could not have if it were shot through the lip of an archangel.

He concluded that it is useful in generating influence to put people of the same class or condition together (women, men, the young, etc.), because "level lines of influence are strongest"[18]—better, presumably, than the trajectories from archangels on high.

"Lines of influence," then, emerged from the sharing of experience, in prayer when one related aloud one's own troubles or one's petitions on behalf of others, and in testimony when telling of the previous religious experiences of self or others. Yet the sharing was virtually anonymous; it was neither likely nor important that those attending a meeting knew one another, nor was it the intent of the revivals to encourage close friendships. Rather, the prayers and conversion accounts articulated the like mindedness, the like feelings, of people unknown to each other. As such, they came to employ a standard language and describe a standard course, thus providing exemplary models of right feeling and right states of mind. This again is an example of how the forms of expression give shape to emotions in a controlled fashion, through conventional formulas. The following prayer requests are typical:

> Pray for a young man who has been in deep darkness and strong temptation, so that he has had thoughts of drowning himself, but has now found his way to the inquiry meetings.[19]

> An anxious wife is praying earnestly at this hour for her husband, who once made a profession of religion, but is

> now fearful that he never was born of the Spirit, and is in darkness. She asks for an interest in your prayers in his behalf.[20]

The formula is: darkness and temptation, often accentuated by breakdowns or suicidal impulses (we may recall Joe Morgan and Mr. Bruder in Arthur's and Roe's novels), from which the person is saved by his or her own prayer, or the prayerful influence of another. Often in testimonies the scenario is more vivid and dramatic, especially if embellished by a good storyteller, as in the following testimony recounted by Moody:

> The man who got up in the prayer meeting . . . said with his business [of rum selling] he hadn't prospered—he failed, and went away to the Rocky Mountains. Life became a burden to him and he made up his mind that he would go to some part of the mountains and put an end to his days. He took a knife with him which he proposed driving into his heart. . . . He heard a voice—it was the voice of his mother. He remembered her words when she was dying, even though he was a boy then. He heard her say "Johnny, if ever you get into trouble, pray to God." That knife dropped from his hand, and he asked God to be merciful to him. He was accepted, and he came back to Chicago and lifted up his voice for Him.[21]

Again, we see the sort of scenario familiar from *Barriers Burned Away* in the death of Dennis's father.

Fear and temptation followed by conversion and peace are, of course, a variation on a long-standing convention. It is important, however, that these emerge within standardized forms of social prayer and testimony, in a carefully orchestrated revival meeting. Even more significant, given our analysis in Chapter 4, is the model in terms of which the events are conceived. It is wholly typical that it is the anxious wife praying for an erring husband, and that it was the memory of his mother that saved the former rum seller. In case after case, it is the *domestic* "lines of influence" that are strongest. People prayed for other objects: the furthering of God's kingdom, the secular government, the salvation of degenerate groups like sailors and stable keepers.[22] But mothers praying for wayward sons, and sons converted because of their mothers, were the favorite circumstances of religious experience—with wife/husband, sister/brother, and child/parent (especially father) coming in close behind.[23] The domestic circle represented the epitome of sympathizing, saving influences. Henry Fish, citing Albert Barnes (a Finneyite) as his authority, defended the workings of "sympathy" in revivals through the pleadings of a father or mother or the tears of a sister, because God uses the natural sympathetic framework of the family to accomplish his purposes. "These sympathies," Fish quotes, referring to familial influences, "are the precious remains of the joys of paradise lost. . . . They serve to distinguish man, though fallen, from the dissocial and unsympathizing apostasy of beings of pure malignancy in hell."[24] The family circle is the prime example of a *social* arena of *like feeling,* united through common joys, sorrows, and sufferings, and mutual love among the members. For that reason its personae and the relationships among them provided the paradigm of religious experience as expressed through prayer and testimony. Right feeling took the form of locating oneself, metaphorically if not actually, within a family circle.

This kind of religious language had by 1875 affected even the sermon, the last stronghold of the Puritan religious heritage. Judging from some sermons of the 1857–58 period preached in New York, most ministers at that time still retained the old style of text, doctrine, and application, although with greater flexibility. Most still emphasized doctrine rather than a personal relationship to Jesus or to family members.[25] In 1875, however, Moody was charming his audiences with a style more like that of a lay exhorter—appropriately enough, since Moody himself was a layman.[26] Contemporaneous commentators noted two main differences between Moody's style and that of other preachers. First, there was Moody's method of "Bible reading," which he probably learned from Henry Moorhouse, a traveling evangelist from the British Plymouth Brethren sect, and from that group's commentaries and tracts.[27] It consisted of choosing a topic—"promises" or "the blood"—and then with the aid of a popular concordance finding all the biblical references which bore on the topic, and finally synthesizing them into one coherent and evangelical interpretation. The second distinctive feature of Moody's style was his use of anecdotes from "daily life," and especially from the paradigmatic situation of home and family.

Whenever he could, Moody gave his characters homes and families or lamented the lack of them. His favorite stories revolved around the relationship of mother and child or child and parent, and especially a dying mother or child. The following is a typical example:

> A family in a Southern city were stricken down by yellow fever. . . . The father was taken sick and died and was buried, and the mother was at last stricken down. The neighbors were afraid of the plague, and none dared to go into the house. The mother had a little son and was . . . afraid he would be neglected when she was called away, so she called the little fellow to her bedside, and said, "My boy, I am going to leave you, but Jesus will come to you when I am gone." The mother died, the cart came along and she was laid in the grave. . . . [The boy] wandered

> about and finally started up to the place where they had laid his mother and sat down on the grave and wept himself to sleep. Next morning . . . a stranger came along and seeing the little fellow sitting on the ground, asked him what he was waiting for. The boy remembered what his mother had told him and answered, "I am waiting for Jesus," and told him the whole story. The man's heart was touched, tears trickled down his cheeks, and he said, "Jesus has sent me," to which the boy replied, "You have been a good while coming, sir."[28]

Another story makes even more explicit the sacrificial and Christ-like character of a mother's death. A mother and son were on a steamer bound for San Francisco, where they were to join the boy's father, when a fire broke out and, because of explosives on board, it was necessary to abandon ship immediately. But the lifeboats were too small:

> In a minute they were overcrowded. The last one was just pushing away, when the mother pled with them to take her and her boy. "No," they said, "we have got as many as we can hold." She entreated them so earnestly, that at last they said they would take one more. . . . She seized her boy, gave him one last hug, kissed him, and dropped him over into the boat. "My boy," she said, "if you live to see your father, tell him that I died in your place."

The point was that if that boy was grateful to his mother, how much more should we be loyal to Christ who died for us; for that story was, Moody said, a "faint type" of his sacrifice.[29] Occasionally, a similar analogy would be used for the male parent, as when Moody told a story about little boys jumping off fenceposts into their father's arms and compared that to the trust men should have in Christ. But when he made his appeal, "Let Jesus touch you to-night," the analogy was that of a mother's loving, tender hand on the brow of her dying son.[30]

Moody well knew that not all families had stalwart fathers and sympathetic mothers, and the broken family, especially when described in terms of the orphaned or ill-treated child, provided an important set of negative symbols. Such a child often became a saintly figure, but usually by coming under the influence of a woman who provided love and compassion. One stubborn little boy was won over, Moody said, to a religious life by the kindness of a young lady who taught Sunday school. His father flogged him for coming to the mission school—for the family was Catholic—but he continued coming to see his teacher. Finally the boy was killed, his legs crushed under the wheels of a train, but he lived long enough to send a message to his parents that he died a Christian. Violent death had purified the boy, but the real hero, as Moody told the story, was the young lady who converted him.[31] She was in effect a surrogate mother, representing what his family should have done for him. In Moody's vision, the family was not only an analogue but the actual means of salvation. In a sermon on "Noah and the Deluge," where the family had been used throughout as the contemporary analogue to the ark, Moody finally entreated:

> Will you not to-night go home and erect a family altar, and call your children around you, and call them to come into the ark, and so you may gather them all in, and you will have them with you when the morning of the Resurrection shall come, and when Christ shall come to make up his jewels?[32]

The family, centered on the figures of mother and child, was the ideal and real model of Christian salvation.

Prayers, testimonies, and sermons in Moody's style all used the domestic image in ways parallel to the popular evangelical novels. But there are interesting differences between revival prayer and testimony on the one hand, and Moody's anecdotes on the other. The personal prayers and accounts emphasized internal turmoil, fear and temptation, the threat of insanity, Moody's anecdotes, on the other hand, emphasized the external world as symbolic of turmoil and strife.[33] One of the common metaphors used in his stories was the city—a familiar convention in evangelical rhetoric since the 1830s at least—but Moody exploits it more fully. Many of his anecdotes have an urban setting: "I met a man in Chicago. . ." or "On the streets of Glasgow.. . ." The formula of the country bumpkin in the big city was standard fare, as in the following account of a farmer who sent his son to sell his crop of grain in Chicago:

> One day, when church business engaged him, he sent his son to Chicago with grain. He waited and waited for his boy to return, but he did not come home. At last he could wait no longer, so he saddled his horse and rode to the place where his son had sold the grain. He found that he had been there and got the money for his grain; then he began to fear that his boy had been murdered and robbed. At last, with the aid of a detective, they tracked him to a gambling den, where they found that he had gambled away the whole of his money. In hopes of winning it back again, he then had sold his team, and lost that money too. He had fallen among thieves, and like the man who was going to Jericho, they stripped him, and then they cared no more about him.

From that day the young man became "a wanderer on the face of the earth," and his father followed "from city to city," seeking him.[34] The analogy is with Jesus seeking to save the lost, but more important for our purposes is the set of associations with the city, not unlike those in Roe's novel: a den of thieves, a place where no one cared about the boy, the site of a fall from innocence into a life of wandering far from home.

A related set of images appears in another story, where the point about the city is made by explicit analogy:

> Look at that man in a boat on Niagara River. He is only about a mile from the rapids. A man on the bank shouts to him, "Young man, young man, the rapids are not far away; you'd better pull for the shore." "You attend to your own business; I will take care of myself," he replies. . . . On he goes sitting coolly in his boat. [A second and a third warning from passersby are ignored.] By and by he says: "I think I hear the rapids—yes, I hear them roar"; and he seizes the oars and pulls with all his strength, but the current is too great, and nearer and nearer he is drawn on to that abyss, until he gives one unearthly scream, and over he goes. Ah, my friends, this is the case with hundreds in this city. They are in the current of riches, of pleasure, of drink, that will take them to the whirlpool.[35]

The city is powerful, threatening, and seductive to the wanderer, and, as the image of the falls and whirlpool suggests, totally out of control. Disaster, in the form of city-as-whirlpool, shipwreck, train accident, disease and death, dominates Moody's description of the world from which people are to be saved.[36] Those sorts of images are familiar to us from the novels. The important point here is that they form a kind of objective correlate to the subjective turmoil and fear recounted in prayer and testimony. The solution to both types of problems, however, lies in the family, especially in the figures of the mother and the child, and for Moody especially through their sacrificial deaths—not unlike Mary Morgan and Ethel Fleet. In the prayers and testimonies, it is the influence of intimate family members which transforms the tumultuous affections into peaceful love; in Moody's stories, it is the mother or child who is stalwart against the threats of the world, an innocent character wandering about in the chaos, ultimately dying in many cases, but preserving a holy influence which has its effect on others.

One more point about Moody's sermons must be made before we return to examine the rhetoric of the hymns. By emphasizing anecdotes, by building his sermons around them, Moody in effect transformed the sermon form into that of testimony. The stories from "daily life," while more vivid than lay narratives, were on a par with them. Moody even used the Bible in this way, retelling the familiar biblical events in a form which made the characters seem down to earth. He fleshed out the characters by giving them families and neighbors, inventing dialogue, comparing them with ordinary people. Often Moody moved from Bible to history and then to the folks next door. In his sermon on "Courage and Enthusiasm," for example, in which he urged Christian workers to keep their eyes on God in order to have courage, he cited the examples of Moses, Elijah, Peter, Noah, and a woman who wanted to fight in the Civil War with a poker as her only weapon; then he moved to Garibaldi, an ancient (unnamed) king, Abe Lincoln, an aged missionary, an eighty-five-year-old London woman, and a fireman saving a child from a burning building.[37] All were examples of courage in the face of overwhelming odds. One might, of course, raise the question whether the progression implied a different valuation of the different periods of human history—a theory of degeneration, perhaps, from the Bible to the present day. But Moody did not always move in such a direct fashion from ancient to modern times; further, he was occasionally explicit about the equality of all periods of history, even though he believed his own generation to be living in the last days. "From Adam's days to ours," he said, "tears have been shed, and a wail has been going up to heaven from the broken-hearted."[38] In history if not in geology, Moody believed in uniformity. His anecdotes about biblical characters and events, just like those of his trips to the British Isles and of fires in Chicago, bore witness to the universality of the kinds of experiences his listeners themselves shared in prayer meeting and inquiry room. As testimonies, they repeated over and over again the same sorts of situations: human beings fearful and weak, wandering aimlessly, threatened by forces beyond their control, including their own passions; yet saved by the calming influence of home and mother or child, by a figure weak or dying but strong and courageous through an intimate relationship to Jesus. Of course Moody was wrong in claiming universality for his interpretation of human nature. It was, as I have shown, the product of a particular cultural situation. But, for Moody as for many religious apologists of the era, a recognition of the diversity of human cultures would not have been congenial to his absolute claims.

This brief survey of the language and conventions employed in the 1857–58 revivals and the Moody-Sankey tour shows that the rhetoric of feeling and the domestic ideal were central to the revivals as well as to the novels. The forms of prayer and testimony dominated, with testimony taking over even the sermon form by Moody's time. The metaphors and conventions are closely parallel to those we identified in the novels and, at the end of Chapter 4, compared with the hymn metaphors. Again we might schematize the revival material, for the sake of convenience, in terms of contrasting sets:

Negative	versus	Positive
City, money-making		Country, home, family, mother, child
Fear, sorrow, wailing		Love, sympathy, peace
Whirlpool, shipwreck, wandering		Lifeboat, shore
Weakness, temptation		Strength in apparent weakness, sacrificial death
World		Jesus, salvation

The parallels with the images of the novels are clear (see Chapter 4), and they are fundamentally the same as the predominant metaphors in the gospel hymns. We may recall once more that most of the hymn metaphors dealt with categories similar to those above, especially with negative versus positive emotions, turmoil versus rest, weakness versus strength. All these appear, elaborated and specified for particular contexts, not only in the evangelical novels but also in the forms used in the revivals themselves. The hymns rest upon the foundation of this evangelical domesticity, as do the revivalist prayers, testimonies, and sermons. In each, the turbulent emotions within the individual and the chaotic turmoil of the world outside come to rest in Jesus.

As we observed in comparing hymns with novels, the hymns do not employ specific descriptions of the family circle and of urban life as in Moody's anecdotes, nor do they refer explicitly to the mother as in prayer and testimony. The metaphors are all adapted to and predicated upon Jesus and heaven on the one hand, and "the world" on the other. Part of the reason for that lies in the intended function of the hymns; they were written for use in revivals and religious meetings which were to direct people to Jesus, not to their mothers. Yet the hymnists were using categories parallel to those of the domestic ideology. Are they to be understood then as inventing their images of Jesus or heaven or the world to correspond to their idea of home or its opposite? While one could posit such an intention at a subconscious level, that is not the best way to understand the hymns. Rather, the tradition of hymnody which they knew contained elements which could be appropriated and reworked in that way, which could provide models for constructing the religious world in such a manner. We return here to a matter raised briefly in Chapter 1: it is not that people had a worldview or set of rules "in their heads" and then wrote hymns to conform to it, but rather that they possessed and used as models earlier hymns which presented a persuasive picture of the world—one which was congruent with other similar cultural productions of their time and place.

For example, there was the ever-popular hymn, Charles Wesley's "Jesus, Lover of My Soul," which appeared in popular hymnals like those of Leavitt and Hastings, and which we have also seen in Roe's novel:

> Jesus, Lover of my soul,
> Let me to Thy bosom fly
> While the nearer waters roll,
> While the tempest still is high;
> Hide me, O my Saviour, hide,
> Till the storm of life is past;
> Safe into the haven guide,
> Oh, receive my soul at last.
>
> (GH 721, 727)

Within one brief compass, we find the metaphors of Jesus as an intimate, the Savior (and heaven) as a haven, and life as a tempest. Nineteenth-century hymnists could imitate that type of hymn, or focus on just one of the metaphors and write an entire hymn around that, or invent other variations. What is distinctive is that they were selecting those kinds of metaphors more frequently than the ones in, say, most of Watts's hymns. They could also turn to various portions of the Bible as sources for appropriate, congruent ideas; one need only think of the extensive use of metaphors of "refuge" in the Psalms. Further, there is clear evidence of imitation even within the popular hymnody of the nineteenth century. "Almost Persuaded" calls forth "Fully Persuaded"; "Tell Me the Old, Old Story" was virtually repeated by the same author in "I Love to Tell the Story"; "Just As I Am" produced the refrain, "Just as thou art." Augustus Toplady's eighteenth-century "Rock of Ages" was progenitor of many "Rock" songs and choruses, while the nineteenth-century novel *The Gates Ajar* soon had a descendant in a hymn of the same name.[39] Examples could be multiplied. The important point is the selection of elements from previous tradition which, while at one level being mere imitation, has new meaning in the context of emerging nineteenth-century language and forms. The significant language context is the ideology of evangelical domesticity and the forms of the community of feeling, especially prayer and testimony.

This does not imply, however, that the hymns merely reflected a prevailing social and ideological situation, i.e., the separation of masculine and feminine spheres reflected in the corresponding metaphors of the evil world versus home. That correspondence is important, yet an interpretation only in such terms would be insufficient. The baseline of the hymn language is the interpretation of the world in terms of emotions. Their aim is to organize the world in those terms, to put passion in its place. This may not be immediately clear from a simple listing of the various polarities. There is a dichotomy of emotions, of course, but the other metaphors—turmoil versus rest, for example, which seem to be directly symbolic of the world/home dichotomy—appear to have the same status. We are here dealing with a crucial question in the analysis of religious ideology, which so often seems to be merely a reflection of some other kind of ideology or of some social situation. The problem appears often because scholars treat religion as composed of belief systems—systems which the scholars have constructed—rather than as it appears in the forms which are its vehicles. That is why I have emphasized throughout the importance of the forms which articulate experience: prayer, testimony, sermon, the hymn itself which uses those while also adding a poetic and musical dimension. The hymn *forms* reveal the fundamental importance of the emotional categories and the articulation of the passions and affections. Prayer, testimony and exhortation, as I showed in Chapter 3, are the fundamental forms of "social religion" whose aim is the creation of a community of feeling. They are strategies which create "lines of influence" and models for the experience of others. Further, if my interpretation of Moody's sermons is correct, his anecdotes fulfilled precisely the same purposes. We must understand the gospel hymns in the same way: their primary import is the way they function to create a sacred community articulated in terms of shared emotions. The analogue of that community is home-and-mother, but the revival community itself is also the sacred community, and as such it does not "reflect" anything other than itself—however much it may draw on analogues to describe and understand itself. The domestic analogue thus must be understood in terms of its function as a model for the control of feeling, the control of the passions which had run wild in the early nineteenth-century revivals. Thanks to domesticity, social religion had finally been tamed, the waves of emotion purified in the fires of hearth and home. The evocation of domestic images, repeated again and again, reinforced the taming of the spirit in prayer and testimony.

The "social religion" context, with its aim of creating a community of controlled feeling, appears clearly in the way gospel hymns were integrated into the revival meetings by the time of Moody and Sankey. The two evangelists used hymns not only to open and close a service but also to parallel each of its segments. Prayer, sermon, testimony, and invitation (altar call) were each preceded or followed by an appropriate hymn. Further, the flexibility of the hymn form, with its various verses and chorus, allowed the different forms to be combined. An example is S. O'Maley Cluff's "I Am Praying For You":

> I have a Saviour, He's pleading in glory,
> A dear, loving Saviour tho' earth friends be few;
> And now He is watching in tenderness o'er me,
> But oh, that my Saviour were your Saviour too.
>
> [Verses follow with "I have a Father," "a robe," "a peace."]
>
> When Jesus has found you, tell others the story
> That my loving Saviour is your Saviour too;
> Then pray that your Saviour may bring them to glory,
> And pray'r will be answered—'twas answered for you!
>
> CHORUS:
> For you I am praying, For you I am praying,
> For you I am praying, I'm praying for you.
>
> (GH 589)

The hymn testifies, entreats, gently exhorts, and prays, combining all the forms of social religion. It emphasizes the commonality of experience, and provides a paradigm for imitation, in counterpoint to the chorus's emphasis on prayer.

Doctrinal hymns of the sort found in Watts's collections are virtually absent from the gospel hymns. They have been replaced by testimonial hymns, as we observed in Chapter 2, but also by some "story hymns" which Sankey made famous. They were designed to accompany Moody's sermons and, as such, complemented his anecdotal, testimonial style. As one commentator observed of Sankey, "His singing is a sort of musical oratory."[40] That oratory frequently took the form of Bible stories translated into hymn form, as in the famous "The Ninety and Nine" (GH 570), a dramatic account of Jesus the Good Shepherd seeking a wayward lamb, or the equally popular "Jesus of Nazareth Passeth By," which is Sankey's version of the story of Jesus healing a blind man in Luke 18:35–38:

What means this eager, anxious throng,
Which moves with busy haste along,
These wondrous gath'rings day by day?
What means this strange commotion pray?
In accents hush'd the throng reply:
"Jesus of Nazareth passeth by."

Who is this Jesus? Why should He
The city move so mightily?
A passing stranger, has He skill
To move the multitude at will?
Again the stirring tones reply:
"Jesus of Nazareth passeth by."

Jesus! 'tis He who once below
Man's pathway trod, 'mid pain and woe;
And burdened ones, where'er He came,
Brought out the sick, and deaf, and lame,
The blind rejoiced to hear the cry:
"Jesus of Nazareth passeth by."

Again He comes! From place to place
His holy footprints we can trace.
He pauseth at our threshold—nay,

He enters—condescends to stay.
Shall we not gladly raise the cry—
"Jesus of Nazareth passeth by?"

Ho! all ye heavy-laden, come!
Here's pardon, comfort, rest, and home.
Ye wanderers from a Father's face,
Return, accept His proffered grace.
Yet tempted ones, there's refuge nigh,
"Jesus of Nazareth passeth by."

But if you still this call refuse,
And all His wondrous love abuse,
Soon will He sadly from you turn,
Your bitter prayer for pardon spurn.
"Too late! too late!" will be the cry—
"Jesus of Nazareth *has passed by*."

(GH 9)

Such hymns were applauded for their vivid portrayals, just as were Moody's sermons; an English writer observed, "the solemn and magnificent songs, seem now to bring Jesus of Nazareth right down into the streets of our own city, or, again, to take us right up to the gates of heaven."[41] Like the sermons, Sankey's solos brought the Bible characters down to the level of daily life, transforming Bible and doctrine into testimony and invitation.

In form, then, the hymns reenacted the revival itself, providing a chorus to it at every point. Its prayers and testimonies and exhortations gave shape to the forms of feeling just as did the petitions of individuals and the narratives of Moody, in fully authorized versions: the *gospel* hymn itself. The hymns added a further dimension to the organization of social affections, however, for they were set to music. In the prevailing conceptions of the nineteenth century, that implied that they "naturally" expressed feeling. Sometimes that sort of assumption was elaborated into a complex theory of musical effects, with different emotions being associated not only with tempo and scale (for example, major versus minor), as is familiar to us, but even with the various keys (C, G, etc.) in which a piece was written.[42] More often, however, one finds simply the assertion that music has the power to awaken deep affections. "Poetry and song," wrote Charles L. Thompson when speaking of revival music, "are the natural language of strong feeling; it falls as easily into rhythmical and musical forms, as logic shapes itself into closely articulated prose."[43] The hymns could thus be said to raise the powers of prayer and testimony to a higher degree. Fish wrote in his handbook of revivals that hymns were capable of "stirring the mind" by arousing mental associations—with, for example, other occasions when a certain hymn was sung. But also, he continued,

> . . . there is a deeper philosophy in it. God is pleased to accompany it [music] with the energy of the Holy Spirit. He made us to be moved by singing. The soul is a many-stringed lyre, which he touches while working in us. Hence, the influence of sacred song is to refresh, stimulate, and ennoble the mind.[44]

Hymns thus occupied a special place, according to their proponents, in the powers of "energy" and "influence" which surrounded the religious life. They also united and elevated the people as a body, as in Thompson's description of a meeting where Eben Tourjée brought a two-thousand-voice choir to a series of Sankey meetings: "the great congregations were nightly led in swelling the great tide of song that swept heavenward, bearing precious souls upward on its great billows of holy emotion."[45] Metaphors like "tide" and "billows" in other contexts (like the world as stormy sea), could apply to objects of fear; here, sanctified by the power of the gospel song, they portrayed the common social energy generated in a revival audience.

In terms of its forms, then, *Gospel Hymns* can be seen as a culmination of the development of social religion, using its major features of prayer, testimony, and exhortation plus music, to create a community of feeling. The nature of religious community had been greatly transformed since the time of the Puritans; it was a group of people whose only likeness (according to the ideology) was likemindedness, like feeling. Fish could write in 1874 what would have been anathema a hundred years earlier: the church was not "a great corporate body" but "only a company of individuals."[46] *Gospel Hymns* was the rhetoric of a company of pilgrims, united only by their common pathway, celebrating their journey, calling others to join the march, and anticipating their goal—although the Moody-Sankey revivals were really a pilgrimage in reverse, since they came to you rather than you going to it. The ties among the individuals in this social body were apparently impermanent and unstable; nevertheless they were intended to be a pervading "influence," a source of strength in time of trouble, just as was the family and the memory of tender maternal affections, in a world of chaos. The hymns constructed an edifice on the values represented by the domestic ideology in order to emphasize the power of Jesus as haven from the world and source of strength to face it—strength gained by being in relationship to a power of strong feeling, passionate yet passive, bounded and controlled, like all the tender feminine affections.

The hymns had an additional value: they did not require even the temporary and transitory structures of the revival meeting, prayer meeting, or inquiry group for their performance; they could be sung anywhere. *Gospel*

Hymns was in a sense a complete portable revival, containing all its forms and figures in melodies which could float upon the air. One Scottish observer rhapsodized in this vein about the impact of the gospel hymns on his land:

> In the remote Highland glen you may hear the sound of hymn-singing; shepherds on the steep hillsides sing Mr. Sankey's hymns while tending their sheep; errand boys whistle the tunes as they walk along the streets of the Highland towns; while in not a few of the lordly castles of the north they express genuine feeling.[47]

The community of feeling could be anywhere, at any time, and could extend over any distance. In terms of structures, it would be difficult to identify such a community at all, or at least that is how it is intended to appear. The community was externally structureless, united only in spirit. One of Sankey's stories brings this home concretely:

> Along the streets of Glasgow, shortly after our first visit to Scotland, a little boy passed one evening, singing "There is a fountain filled with blood." A Christian policeman joined in the song, and when he had finished his beat he asked the boy if he understood what he was singing. "Oh, yes," said the little fellow, "I know it in my heart, and it is very precious." A few evenings afterward some one asked the policeman: "Do you know that a woman standing where we are was awakened and saved the other night by hearing 'There is a fountain,' sung by a policeman and a boy?"[48]

Here we find no church, no minister, not even a revival tabernacle. The actors are virtually anonymous, although one is a child, an emblem of domesticity and purity. The locale is on the streets of a city, the symbol of worldliness.

The singers meet by chance and sing together, to no one in particular but, by virtue of the hymn itself, creating their own temporary community of feeling. As chance would have it, the notes of the hymn work on the soul of a passerby; its words and the words of the child provide a testimony to a "precious" truth, a model and an implicit entreaty, and she is transformed. The hymn itself, apart from other religious forms and structures but given life by the singing pilgrims, touched the many-stringed lyre of a human heart. We may recall Fanny Crosby's famous lines:

> Down in the human heart,
> Crush'd by the tempter,
> Feelings lie buried that grace can restore;
> Touched by a loving heart,
> Wakened by kindness,
> Chords that were broken will vibrate once more.
> (GH592.3)

The gospel-hymn rhetoric is indeed a unique strategy, one which appropriates the resources of a particular religious tradition and a dominant popular ideology, and shapes them into forms which articulate a particular kind of religious community. In this respect the revivalist rhetoric differs from that of the liberal clergy discussed by Ann Douglas. Whereas for the latter the adoption of the domestic ideology signaled a retreat into a private sphere, the evangelicals projected the domestic ideal back outward again, into the public or rather "social" arena of revivals. That does not mean they contributed more to the intellectual or political tradition—quite the contrary, for the revivalist orientation was more otherwordly than that of its liberal counterpart and thus promoted premillennial and conservative tendencies. What is does mean is that the revival itself provided a broader community of active participation which reinforced the tradition. Unfortunately, the implications of the revivalist rhetoric were as questionable as that of their liberal brothers and sisters. Its emphasis on likeness of feeling glorified uniformity and homogeneity; its uncritical appropriation of the domestic ideology contributed to the isolation of home and woman in a separate sphere—a sacred one, to be sure, but therefore divorced from the rest of life. By denying any significance other than a negative one to outward structures such as the institutions of nineteenth-century urban life, it discouraged efforts at legal and political reform of the larger society. The reduction of all significant knowledge to testimony about individuals' emotional states made it virtually impossible to gain a wider perspective on the Bible or on theological issues. Most important for our purposes, the creation of a community of feeling which claimed to be purely religious and to transcend the mundane world disguised the uses to which the rhetoric could be put. The notion that deep in their hearts all people were essentially the same—and if they were not they were evil, insane, or otherwise perverted—concealed the fact that it was only a particular group of people who thought and felt that way. The rhetoric could be employed to create a community which claimed no political or structural ties, while in fact being deeply implicated in social and political identities. In the next chapter I will show how this was indeed the case.

6

Social Religion and Passionate Politics: The Situation of the Hymns

THE rhetoric of the gospel hymns aimed at creating a community of feeling made up of individuals who had "put passion in its place," who had domesticated their affections and thereby purified their lives. They were intimately tied to Jesus and on their way to heaven by virtue of the power of the home circle, and bound to one another and to God by the mutual "lines of influence" generated from their common inner experiences. We have seen in Chapter 4 that the original situation out of which this rhetorical strategy emerged was the separate sphere created by women and clergy, through the vehicle of popular literature. In their novels of evangelical domesticity, they had portrayed themselves as inhabitants of a sacred realm set apart from the world, but also as the source of redemptive power for men who remained part of the evil world. Rhetorically, the gospel-hymn lyrics are part of this development. Yet in the latter half of the nineteenth century the hymns came to the fore in widespread revivals which extended their appeal. Clearly, these revivals were not just for women. The 1857–58 revival attracted middle-class businessmen in all the major Northern cities for lunch-hour meetings. In 1875–77, Moody and Sankey made a strong appeal to men in the urban centers. That they felt a need to emphasize this side of the revival, to create special "young men's meetings" for example, may indicate a concern lest the revival attract only women. But it is also the case that they were largely successful: all reports testify that men thronged to the special meetings and to the general public ones. The community of feeling, incarnate in the gospel hymns, thus became persuasive to large numbers of people, male and female alike. Why would that be the case? This is a crucial question, because the success of the revivals of 1857–58 and 1875–77 laid a foundation for a long tradition of hymnody and revivalism, from Moody to Billy Sunday to Billy Graham. Its power was not ephemeral or limited to women and clergy. It became, if not a dominant tradition, certainly a popular option for multitudes of white middle-class Americans of both sexes during the succeeding century.

Because the expansion of the sphere of influence of the gospel hymns seems directly related to their use in the mass revivals, we will consider them together. We want to know the specific context of revival/hymn strategy: in Kenneth Burke's terms, what sort of "situation" did it seek to encompass? Burke's approach to rhetoric as discussed in Chapter 1 suggests that such questions may be tackled by asking about "identification": with whom or what did the revival audiences identify? We can speak only in general terms about their identities: they were white, aspiring middle-class, evangelical Protestant Northerners. By the late 1850s that meant they were also almost by definition Republican, mildly nativist, anti-Catholic, anti-Mormon, sound-money advocates; urban dwellers but in some cases probably rural-born.[1] What we want to know is whether there might be anything in that range of identifications to which the hymn and revival rhetoric might have appealed.

Earlier interpretations of the late nineteenth-century revivals have selected for emphasis the feature that the audiences were relatively new to urban life, essentially country folk come to the city. According to William G. McLoughlin, they were "intellectually unsophisticated, and sentimentally insecure," "fearful and perplexed"; Bernard Weisberger says "they were ready for reassurance, for a *nostalgic* revival."[2] Certainly the audiences were composed of socially mobile groups, perhaps rural-born; but that does not necessarily entail a psychological explanation in terms of anxieties and insecurities. McLoughlin and Weisberger seem to have erred by interpreting revival rhetoric literally, assuming that because the hymns sang of fears and woes and of heaven as home, and because Moody castigated the evils of urban life, the audiences must be longing to return to the farm. But the dichotomy between home and city is a convention which, while surely reflecting some concern about urban life, is not just a psychological reflex but part of a whole cosmology. It is part of a complex understanding of human beings, social reality, and the cosmos in terms of the passions or emotions, the domestic affections versus the worldly impulses.

McLoughlin and Weisberger argue further that the insecure city folk responded to the Moody-Sankey revivals[3] because of the new currents of ideas which threatened their traditional beliefs. The new revivalism was "defensive," shaped "negatively" in reaction to science, materialism, and radicalism; it was the conservative side of what McLoughlin calls the "third great awakening" which also produced new theologies and ecclesiologies in such liberal forms as evolutionism and ecumenicism. As such, revivalism was the product of the age, which in turn was produced by the move from agricultural society to industrial urbanism, from a homogeneous to a polygenetic population, from anticolonialism to imperialism, and a host of related changes.[4] In terms of the social changes cited as causing "the age," it is true that such changes were occurring, and had been for some decades. But to invoke those as explanations hypostatizes the notion of an "age," viewing it as growing or decaying of its own accord as in McLoughlin's most general explanation of the awakenings: "Without such periodic reorientations and reformulations of the cultural ethos, a civilization inevitably dries up and disintegrates."[5] Such a description fails to produce an account of the ongoing activity of world construction. Although some of the generalizations might be reformulated to apply to specific situations, they do not explain the specific strategy of the gospel hymns and urban revival as relevant to the particular situation of the urban North in 1875.

In terms of explaining the revivals as reactions to science, materialism, and radicalism, McLoughlin even admits that his interpretation is anachronistic: "Moody's most successful revivals occurred in the decade from 1873 to 1883 before the full impact of these changes was recognized and given expression. . . . "[6] In fact, while evolutionism was being discussed from time to time in the popular religious press, it had by no means become a central issue; philological and archaeological research had not undermined biblical authority; and concern about radicalism was virtually nonexistent until, at the earliest, the strikes of 1877 when spectres of (say) the 1871 Paris commune rose to greater relevance.[7] Unless we wish to imagine that Moody's revival audiences were composed of prophets and fortunetellers, McLoughlin's and Weisberger's accounts must be rejected. Of course their approaches utterly fail to account for the 1857–58 revival which, as I have shown, was rhetorically very similar to the Moody-Sankey campaign.

We will better understand the context of the revivals by taking more seriously the wider range of identifications mentioned above; the leaders, hymnists, and participants in the revivals were not only urban but also Northern, white middle-class Republicans. It will be objected that these are, broadly speaking, political and economic identifications, whereas the rhetoric of the hymns and revivals is wholly apolitical. That is true; yet it is quite possible that an apolitical strategy might emerge to deal with a disturbing political situation. A further problem is raised by McLoughlin's statement that there is no relation between revivalism and political matters: "There is no meaningful correlation . . . between the great national awakenings in America and the great periods of political or economic crisis. Neither wars, nor depressions, nor critical elections have produced revivals."[8] In my judgment, McLoughlin's statement is either misconceived or patently in error, as far as the mainstream of late nineteenth-century Northern revivalism is concerned. The great revivals *were* contemporaneous with major political crises: the 1857–58 revival with the heated antislavery crisis and the rise of Republicanism; and the great Moody revivals of 1875–77 with the end of Reconstruction, a crisis caused by political corruption, the resurgence of the Democratic party, and a disputed and finally stolen election.[9] Indeed, the correlations are so precise that it is surprising they have been overlooked.

The revival of 1857–58 ought to have been the obvious case. The nation was inflamed over sectional disputes, had just been inundated with the first great wave of nativism in politics, and was on the brink of war. In that situation, a revival that swept the Northern cities could hardly have been a mere diversion. The Compromise of 1850, the Fugitive Slave Law, and the Kansas-Nebraska bill, permitting expansion of slavery into the free territories, outraged Northern antislavery men. The new political parties, Republican and American ("Know-Nothings," a nativist group), split the non-Democratic vote in 1856, allowing Buchanan to win the Presidency. The Dred Scott decision of 1857 seemed to abrogate the rights of all Northerners to freedom in their own states, and the Northern press charged again and again that the "Slave Power" was running the country even up to the highest judiciary.[10] Then the panic of 1857 crippled business, and soon the revival was under way.

McLoughlin states that the panic was the cause of the revival, "as everyone recognized at the time";[11] but that, as he admits, would make it unique among revivals. The factors involved are more complex. Concern over slavery had been increasing for the previous decade, and more voices were agreeing with the radical abolitionists of earlier years that the institution was a national sin, a notion enforced by Stowe's *Uncle Tom's Cabin.* Portraits of the slave system in the South increasingly emphasized not only its political tyranny but also its perversion of the family, and therefore of the minds and hearts of whites as well as of blacks. It was the antithesis of the Northern system of "free labor," and now its corruption was threatening even the free states. There was also a deep concern about the Northern system itself, which Southerners had attacked as "wage slavery," and for its people's total preoccupation with acquisitiveness.[12] In that context, the panic of 1857 seemed a proof of the Southern charges. The North was sinful not only for acquiescing in the existence of slavery but also for its wild passion for money. An 1858 editorial in the *Independent,* an influential Congregationalist paper, reflected that interpretation:

> As a people we had grown torpid under that crime ["the aggressions of slavery"] for which God so often visited

> Israel with judgments; but the atrocious doings of the Slavepower at Washington and in Kansas aroused the people of God to repentance, to watchfulness, to prayer, and thus prepared the way for God to visit us again with mercy. The sin of luxury He rebuked by the mysterious Providence that subverted our commerce, and so the pride of man was humbled that the grace of God might enter.[13]

The revival was thus a strategy of purification, through repentance of individuals from the national sins of aggressiveness and lust for money. The community, understood as "a people," had to be cleansed, and this was done through the revival which brought individuals into the proper state of mind.

The concerns of the revival went beyond this, however. If the revival were to purge all sins in order to restore the proper community of feeling and morality, there were other difficulties to be overcome. Besides slavery, two other important and highly divisive issues had complicated the 1850s. One was the temperance cause, which had been powerful enough to win the enactment of a prohibition law in Maine in 1851, but then after a few small victories had declined and finally had been ignored in the 1856 Republican platform. The other was nativism, which had surfaced in the American party but also disappeared from Republican politics. In light of those considerations, it is remarkable that in the reports from the 1857–58 revival there are three kinds of conversions (or rededications perhaps) which recur again and again: the turning of men from their preoccupation with business affairs, which of course relates to the general sin of acquisitiveness; second, the reform of drunkards; and third, the conversion of Roman Catholics.[14] The latter two received emphasis, I would argue, because they represented evils which might have divided the Northern evangelicals but which were overcome by the people turning to Jesus. Even if the majority of participants were not those sorts of sinners repenting, it is still of utmost importance that the publicity about the revivals portrayed them that way. The nation was rhetorically, metaphorically, and ritually turning from the sins which it had committed and which threatened its unity as a community of feeling. The evangelicals could regard their community as cleansed not only because its members gave up their chief, ubiquitous sin, but also because the anomalous and potentially threatening elements—alcoholics and Catholics, both slaves to evil passions and alien powers—were being reformed and brought to a proper level of feeling. Further, the revivals were confined to Northern cities, a fact frequently noted by commentators. Accounts of the revival seldom mentioned the South. It represented the alien power, not purified by the movements of the Spirit.

The general political situation, if understood in terms of "identification" and not party politics alone, thus has considerable bearing on our understanding of revivalism. In some ways that should come as no surprise. In the traditional criticisms of worldliness, business with its lust and politics with its clamor and strife were prime objects of attack. Further, the "otherworldliness" of revivalism had never been complete. The sphere of the religious, like that of the home, was an enclave *in* the world which was a channel for spirituality, a pipeline or telegraph wire from heaven through which blessings could flow throughout society. As we saw in Chapter 3, too, the boundaries between the religious-moral-social and political spheres could be gerrymandered in one direction or another from time to time. Evangelical culture, from the beginning of the nineteenth century onward, was ambivalent in its relations to politics. The church, and religious organizations, could not directly participate as entities in the political process, but if issues could be formulated in moral-social terms, if they could be understood in terms of right or wrong structures of the emotional life, religious people were in a sense bound to act, and churchmen to speak out, using their "influence" wherever possible to persuade others.

Nor was that view confined to denominations with a theocratic heritage. In 1875 a Methodist newspaper proclaimed the necessity of a relation of religion to politics in an article whose general aim, paradoxically, was to condemn the partisan machinations of the Roman Catholic Church:

> There may be moral questions involved in politics—slavery was such a question, and the liquor traffic is another—and on these, individual Christians, local churches, and ecclesiastical bodies may express opinions and urge measures, without just cause of complaint. The action is public, is well understood, is peculiar to no sect, and aims at no sectarian advantage. The object is moral and not political, and can be promoted by all religious bodies alike.[15]

The lack of awareness that some religious bodies, such as the Roman Catholic one, might not agree on issues such as temperance appears remarkable; but the evangelical assumption of uniformity was very strong. This meant that moral issues could seem divorced from "sectarian" interests. Religious newspapers of the day were not strictly devotional but, like their earlier predecessors before the era of the great secular dailies, commented on all kinds of current issues, political and economic ones included. Conversely, religious people might well be politically active, given the intensity of political organization in the period.[16] Often the only thing that separated evangelical religion from politics is the fact that churches did not form official political parties. Evangelicals clearly believed that one could and sometimes should try to change people's political behavior, when moral issues were involved, by changing their hearts.

In that light, we can understand the great revivals of 1857–58 as methods of maintaining society through the hearts of its people, creating in them proper levels of feeling under just the right "temperature" control, to borrow Finney's metaphor; that would in turn ensure proper moral behavior. As thermostats of a sort, revivals were techniques of what Jonathan Smith has called "rectification."[17] The ideal was a free society of working people, each pursuing his own interests and enterprises without encroaching on others; all would be morally pure individuals not given to extremes. When society became too hot or too cold, when individuals revealed their more vulgar passions, an adjustment was necessary. Of course there are numerous possible variations on this theme. The more extreme evangelicals (and sociologically one would expect them to be associated with marginal groups) would tend to see the church or society as "cold" or "dead," as indeed Finney had done. In the temperance movement, the revival could become an instrument to cool down the hotheaded drunkards. In the great national revivals we find a situation in which society as a whole was regarded as overheated with passion, therefore evil and corrupt. In such a situation, people in large numbers found denuciations of sin to be persuasive, to be in fact descriptive of the chaos in which they lived. They responded by renewing their own dedication and attempting to convince others of the necessity of reformation. Reformation meant a reform of the heart, a closer walk with Jesus, so that moral reform could be generated from within. That was the aim of the revival rhetoric.

This, however, raises a further question: what brought

large numbers of people to such a point? There must have been, I would suggest, not only the consciousness of a need for internal purification of individual and community, but also a threat from what was perceived as an alien power, one which threatened the balance of passions. *Self*-purification was performed in order to define one's own community as *different from* the aliens. The religious transcendence of the revival was also, to return to a suggestion I made in Chapter 1, a sociological transcendence. This, of course, is a factor operating at a level not fully conscious. But it seems clear that in the 1857–58 revival all the strategies were designed to create a homogeneous community in the North over against the Slave Power which had somehow gotten in control. Despite the intentions of the Northerners, who had thought slavery could be contained, the *wrong* people—people of an aristocratic, parasitical, and aggressive temperament—had seized the reins of government and intended to spread their pernicious system throughout the land. The situation could only be rectified, from an evangelical perspective, by inward purification to ensure a reformation of morals and appropriate political action. The revival was their instrument for that task. The election of Lincoln could be seen as its fulfillment.

Much the same kind of analysis can be applied to the 1875–77 revivals. The country was in the last years of Reconstruction, and the focus of concern was on conditions in the South and on the political corruption of the era. In 1871 the Tweed Ring of the Democratic party in New York had been exposed in a campaign by the *New York Times* and *Harper's Weekly,* illuminated by the famous cartoons of Thomas Nast. Trouble was brewing in the Republican party too, however, As a great war hero, Ulysses S. Grant had been elected President in 1868, but soon corruptions in his administration were revealed. Dissatisfaction with Radical Reconstruction led to a defection from the party of the Union by liberal reformers in 1872. Then, in the fall of 1873, there was a panic, blamed on the Gould and Fisk scandals of a few years before; the panic created a serious depression and an increasing clamor for monetary reform. Especially, the government was accused of defaulting on its promises to resume specie payments on wartime greenbacks. Exposures of Republican corruption had continued, and by 1874 the party's reputation was so bad that Democrats won control of the House of Representatives for the first time since 1859. In 1875 the exposure of the Whiskey Ring, climaxing in the indictment of Grant's personal secretary, convinced even most diehards (since many had continued to believe in the President's righteousness) that Grant was not untainted. The evangelical world was shaken when Henry Ward Beecher of Plymouth Church in Boston, the country's most popular preacher, was accused and brought to trial (1874–75) for adultery by the husband of one of his parishioners. When in 1874 James Russell Lowell sent back from Europe a poem describing his native country as a "Land of Broken Promises," it was widely reprinted; and nearly everyone, whether their concern was sound money or sexual morality, could agree.[18]

One other issue of a different sort was occupying the attention of the public press in the urban North, namely "the school question." In the late 1860s Roman Catholic groups had begun pressuring local governments for tax funds for parochial schools and for removing the (Protestant) Bible from use in public schools. The issue had come to a head especially in Cincinnati, Ohio, where in 1870 the Superior Court ruled against the Board of Education which had prohibited religious instruction and religious books in the common schools. In 1873, however, the Ohio Supreme Court reversed the ruling, a victory for the Catholic partisans.[19] That increased animosities in many quarters, and in 1875 Rutherford B. Hayes used the issue extensively in his successful Ohio gubernatorial campaign, linking Catholics with the Democratic party. Grant, too, hinted at the possibility of religious conflict if sectarianism could not be kept out of the public schools.[20]

The issue did not become a dominant one in the 1876 presidential campaign. Yet, while this upsurge of nativism was shortlived, it occurred at a crucial time and was very widespread. Week after week, the popular religious newspapers discussed various dimensions of Catholicism and its power: its attempts to spread its influence in Europe, its designs on the American government, the claims of the papacy (especially the doctrine of infallibility proclaimed at the Vatican Council of 1870). Moderate papers like the *Independent* assured its readers that there was nothing to worry about, because after all the Catholics in America were gradually becoming Christianized. As for the school question, all that was necessary was to maintain fair play and the Protestants would "vanquish them utterly."[21] If this was a moderate position, one can imagine the more extreme ones. Thomas Nast's cartoons in *Harper's Weekly* throughout 1875 showed the attacks of Catholicism on the nation and, of course, linked it to the Democratic party. One of the most striking drawings (originally printed in 1871 and now reprinted) pictures a group of cardinals as alligators, their miters as open mouths ringed with pointed teeth, slithering up the shore to devour a group of school children while the Tammany Hall gang looks on approvingly. Concurrent articles often linked the Democrats to papal influence, claiming that their party was "the party of ignorance, the party of priests."[22] The *Northwestern Christian Advocate* warned that the tendency of the "Romish" hierarchy to seek political power was endemic: "The virus is in the system, and nothing but death can expel it."[23]

On the one hand, the Republicans and the North in general faced the scandals of "Grantism" in their pure Union party; on the other hand, there was the threat of Catholic power which might be increased under the growing Democratic strength, besides the waning but perhaps still significant fears of a resurgent South. Interwoven with discussions of those matters, intriguing reports filtered in of a revival in Britain, of the English and Scottish and Irish common people and even some of their lords flocking to hear two American evangelists named Moody and Sankey. As their London campaign drew to a close, commentators on the revival looked hopefully toward their return to the States. In a front-page article in the *Independent,* Brooklyn pastor Theodore L. Cuyler expressed a wish for renewal of the nation's spirit in all areas of life:

> The revival, then, which we need is a revival of the religion which keeps God's commandments; which tells the truth and sticks to its promises; which pays twenty shillings to the pound; which cares more for a good character than a fine coat; which votes at the ballot-box in the same direction that it prays; which denies ungodly lusts and which can be trusted in every stress of temptation. A revival which will sweeten our homes and chasten our press and purify our politics and cleanse our business and commerce from roguery and rottenness would be a boon from Heaven. A revival which will bring not only a Bible-knowledge, but a *Bible-conscience* to all is what the land is dying for.[24]

There could hardly be a clearer statement of the sweeping reform hoped for from revival. Economics and politics were to be purified, lusts and temptations were to be overcome. This was not idiosyncratic to Cuyler; the same kinds of sentiments came from the West, in the Methodist Church:

> . . . The developments of the last few years show that a revival of honesty is needed in our land; inside the churches and outside of them. Plainly, the haste to get rich has spread wide demoralization in all ranks. . . . This leads men to speculation as preferable to industry, and it tempts not a few to forms of it which are mere gambling. Then, while one class takes to burglary and highway robbery, a larger class lives by its wits in ingenious fraud practiced on the unsuspecting. . . .
>
> . . . Now, religious reformation should ever have reference . . . to the peculiar vices and dangers of the times.[25]

That quotation makes explicit the relation of the sins of the nation to the traditional sins of the passions, especially the "haste to get rich," which makes people into criminals of one form or another. Speculation becomes "gambling," and all this leads to widespread "demoralization." The tone of the rhetoric is less sweeping, but behind it lurks the concern of Lyman Beecher for order, morality, and civilization. In 1875, however, order was not a matter of social rank; it was a question of individuals correcting their own personal sins, in the inward movement of a revival. The "nation" was now regarded as a community of feeling, which could be purified from within the hearts of its people.

The revivals of the late nineteenth century were, to say the least, not totally divorced from social, political, and economic considerations. They aimed at more than the conversion of individuals, although the individual change of heart was the gateway into social change. The key which unlocked the door between the two was the translation of political issues into moral terms. Slavery became not simply a distinctive political arrangement but a crime of aggression; an economic downturn was not a product of marketing practices but a rebuke for the sin of luxury; financial investments were seen as forms of gambling; monetary policy was reduced to a matter of keeping promises. Voting was the same kind of action as praying, and both were related to the restraint of "ungodly lusts" and the overcoming of "every stress of temptation." By that translation, potentially divisive issues were placed in a framework where all (evangelicals) could agree "in *feeling* and *practice*," as Finney had said, if not in political and economic theory. Direct attacks by churches on the South, the Democratic party, or Grant would have been improper in the context of church-state separation, but by appealing to definitions of social conditions in terms of well-recognized virtues and vices, evangelicals were grounding their commentaries on the broadest sort of "Christian affinity." We can go further: direct political tactics were not only improper, they were unnecessary, for the community to which revivals appealed operated in terms of different structures than party identification or even church membership. All those who evidenced the proper level of feeling—who participated in the warm "sympathy" of a revival meeting and showed control of their "lusts" in their behavior—were part of that community. All those who did not were elements from which the community had to be purified, or over against which it had to be defined—Catholics, drunkards, Southerners, Democrats.

That very specific context for the revivals sheds considerable light on the situation of the gospel hymns. We can account for their immediate impact in terms of the revivals of 1857–58 and 1875–77, which in turn were related to a specific political crisis in which crucial community identifications were at stake. Let us return to the rhetoric of the gospel hymns, very briefly, and consider how we may understand them as "encompassing" this situation. First of all, its forms—comprising prayer, testimony, exhortation, and music—created "social religion," a community based on likeness of feeling. The assumption, from the Finney era onward, was that Christian feeling would generate Christian moral behavior and would, by means of "influence," cleanse a whole community. The community thus created was sacred, nonworldly, for it was concerned only with Jesus and heaven. Yet, as we saw most particularly in the novels but also in the revivals described in Chapter 5, it was to have an effect on moral behavior: people gave up alcohol, helped one another, were honest and gentle, in accord with the feminine idealization on which the community of feeling was based.

The community was transcendent especially in that it stood over against the mundane world, conceived metaphorically as the locus of turmoil and chaos, darkness and wandering, all of which were also metaphors for uncontrolled passions. Individuals were helpless victims of the overpowering forces of the world; they were caught in a whirlpool which could lead only to ruin and death. Those metaphors could provide a cosmic frame for the situations of the late 1850s and mid-1870s. I have argued that one of the crucial conditions of the revivals was a perception of an alien power which threatened the integrity of the community—in 1857, the South as Slave Power; in 1875, the Catholics and Democrats as agents of the Pope. Those were the external factors of evil in the world, the dark forces who wished to take over the system surreptitiously, by extending slavery into free territory or introducing European despotism into America under the guise of a free educational system. In both cases the regular political channels had failed. The highest court had upheld the Fugitive Slave Law in 1857 and the Catholic pressure groups in 1873. In each case the wrong people were in control, people who were believed to be slaves to immorality and evil passions and who now wielded a mysterious power which seemed impossible to conquer.

But there were internal factors of evil as well, sins of passion like acquisitiveness and alcohol looming large among them. If those could be cured, if the internal balance of passions could be restored, there was perhaps hope—if not hope of worldly victory, then at least of heaven. Thus the hymns sought to generate inward strength by turning to Jesus who would provide for all needs in the struggle against the world:

> Take the name of Jesus with you,
> Child of sorrow and of woe—
> It will joy and comfort give you,
> Take it then where'er you go.
>
> Take the name of Jesus ever,
> As a shield from ev'ry snare;
> If temptations 'round you gather,
> Breathe that holy name in prayer.
> (GH 47.1–2)

Further, by singing one could enact and thereby articulate the proper level of feeling, and one could be part of the community that sang. Gathering strength in the "Sweet Hour of Prayer" and then marching forward "Singing All the Time," the revival community, though a group of discrete individuals with no explicit political organization or identity, nevertheless could create self-reinforcing bonds through the articulation of identical emotions. Set to the music of the genteel tradition, the hymns ensured sublimity of feeling, yet controlled, in perfect measure. For the individual, earthly lusts could become a lust for Jesus, and one could cling to him until the final rest which would deliver all right-feeling Christians from the difficulties of this world. Meanwhile, if the world was in turmoil, in the grasp of evil forces, at least there was one pure space, a community washed white as snow.

I am not claiming, of course, that the associations with the political situation were conscious, nor even that the hymns "symbolized" such a situation. The conscious aspects were the perception of immorality within the ranks and danger from outside; the belief that immorality could be cured by revival; and, as I showed in Chapter 5, the recognition of the role of hymns and other revival forms in conversion by changing people's hearts and welding them together. But the connections among all those elements were not made explicit. The hymns did not deal with the political situation directly; they were a strategy for transcending it by defining a sacred community. What we discover through an analysis of the situation is that the transcendence involved also a sociological element, defining *this* community over against *that* one. It was expected that a member of the holy community would act in holy ways—would vote in the same direction that he prayed. But in the hymns themselves, the potential political implications were disguised. It is not even necessary that the members of the revived community of feeling actually did vote in the right direction (in 1860 they did; in 1876 the results were more mixed). The point is that, under the given conditions, the world as perceived was congruent with the world as the hymns portrayed it. One could follow through with the "right" kind of moral and political action, or one could rest content with the hymns' claim to offer a better world, one which transcended all earthly cares. The hymns, which were the result of a long development of rhetorical strategies, in this situation became persuasive for dealing at a cosmic level with what seemed an impossible set of social, political, and economic circumstances.

Having proved their efficacy in difficult situations, the hymns could henceforth become vehicles for articulating a widespread community defined in terms of pure and proper feeling. They did not always have to be political vehicles. The community of feeling, as a portable revival detachable from the structures of mass meetings, could be a home, a church, or an amorphous group which chose to sing together. Once the tradition was established, the hymns could float indefinitely. But evangelicals could also appropriate them as symbols of unity in the face of potential threats from groups perceived as alien, whether aristocratic Southerners or despotic Catholics, or later, Jews or Communists or homosexuals. The popular evangelical tradition has a propensity to see conspiracies lurking around every corner; it is probably no accident that Billy Graham rose to fame in the late 1940s during the Communist scare which culminated in the atrocities of the McCarthy era. Most often evangelicals view the aliens as working through perversion of the passions and subversion of the mind—"brainwashing," or subtly indoctrinating children in the public schools, as in the Catholic question of the 1870s and in the antihomosexual campaign of Anita Bryant, a singing star and evangelical Christian, in the 1970s. In all these cases the nation, which for the most part means white middle-class Protestant Christians, has become from the evangelical perspective a "community of feeling," a form of social religion. Understanding that, we may now be able to perceive more clearly the connection between mainstream evangelicalism and what other scholars have called "civil religion": the inward religion of intimacy with Jesus and the purity exemplified by home, woman, and family, are transformed into civil religion by virtue of "social religion," a community of shared feeling.

There may even be cases in which international implications arise. The late-nineteenth-century community of feeling was not limited to the United States, as is evident from the transatlantic appeal of the revivals of both the 1850s and the 1870s, and from the popularity of Sankey's hymns on both sides of the ocean, Britain as well as America. The connection was again an apolitical identification; yet Rufus Clark in closing his account of the British revivals could express the hope that "the two great Protestant nations of the earth may thus be led to join hands, more cordially than ever before. . . ."[26] The cordial union of Protestant nations was supposed to be a religious act, transcending mere human politics. Yet the aim of the hymns as portable revival was to transform human society, diffusing the gentle influences of social religion unto the ends of the earth—in such a way as to exert "influence" on Catholics and other tyrants, drunkards and other deviants, and, we may imagine, on the "Bulgarians" and "Fejee Islanders" of whom some commentators spoke. Of course the reformation was supported to begin at home. The hymns always insisted on personal piety first and cementing the ties of Christians to one another, but then bringing others into the fold by a simple call to come to Jesus:

Are you coming home, ye wand'rers,
  Whom Jesus died to win,
All footsore, lame and weary
  Your garments stain'd with sin?
Will you seek the blood of Jesus
  To wash your garments white;
Will you trust His precious promise,
  Are you coming Home tonight?
(GH 184.1)

From the Highland glen to the streets of San Francisco, evangelicals sang those same songs and thus were, they believed, bound together by their common inner experience, an experience which would provide strength in all worldly trials and eventually victory by nonworldly, apolitical means, coming Home together. But as we watch Rex Humbard visiting lepers in Korea and Billy Graham condemning "devil-worship" in Brazil—both inviting people of other traditions to give them up for the calm uniformity of the American middle-class home—we might well wonder whether rescue mission has not turned into imperial mission after all.

It may not be appropriate (although there is a certain form of justice in it) to turn the conspiracy theories of popular evangelicalism back on itself. What is important is to gain a critical perspective on the ideas and forms of revivalism which have shaped much of American culture and a great deal of our everyday rhetoric—the idea of the individual's inner states as the key to his character, the "social" as a realm which creates uniformity through bonds of emotion, the segregation of home and woman from the real world, the potential political uses of apolitical rhetoric. The implications of all these need to be re-examined critically, for they are clearly the product of certain groups in certain kinds of social and political situations; they have no *a priori* authority. They demand argument rather than acceptance; and they open up various areas of inquiry for historical-critical studies.

Of course, one might also dismiss this as an occasional mad flurry of "the popular mind," these revivals and hymns and, nowadays, television evangelists. But we ought to remember the *New York Times* writer quoted at the beginning of this book, who tried to dismiss the British revivals by saying simply that in England everybody was mad. The Americans, however, turned out to be mad as well, and intended to remake the world in that kind of insanity. Yet they would have said that they, and they alone, had overcome the many madnesses of the world.

Appendix

Methods of Analyzing the Hymns

It is important in the study of popular literature and culture to be explicit about methods, especially because this is a relatively new field of study. Too often such studies are done impressionistically; or, even when they are not, it is assumed that the methods and categories of analysis are obvious. They are not always obvious; and further, only when they are clearly laid out (even if the clarification is done after the fact) can they be refined, and wrong assumptions corrected. Discussion of methods can be tedious, however, so I have reserved most of the specific techniques of rhetorical analysis for this Appendix.

The category of analysis of the hymns which most needs clarification and justification is that of metaphor. As noted in the text, the gospel hymns and most of the other hymns considered are built around series of metaphors, as in the following:

> Not now, my child,—a little more rough tossing,
> A little longer on the billows' foam;
> A few more journeyings in the desert darkness,
> And then, the sunshine of thy Father's Home!
> (GH 628.1)

One could analyze this one verse as containing seven metaphors: (1) the human being as a child, (2) the world as a stormy sea; (3) life as a journey, (4) world as desert, (5) darkness of the world, (6) light of heaven, and (7) heaven as home. This hymn is unusually compact and complex; more often the metaphors change only from line to line or couplet to couplet. Some hymns are built entirely around one dominant metaphor. In P. P. Bliss's famous "Pull for the Shore," the chorus repeats and elaborates the metaphor of storm-at-sea, with the "shore" as the opposing term:

Pull for the shore, sailor, pull for the shore!
  Heed not the rolling waves, but bend to the oar,
  Safe in the lifeboat, sailor, cling to self no more!
  Leave the poor old stranded wreck, and pull for the shore.
(GH 51.Ch)

Such metaphors are fundamental, repeated structures throughout the hymns. Only Watts's hymns are sometimes an exception, when they take on the character of a condensed doctrinal exposition. That sometimes makes it difficult to translate them exactly into the metaphors of the gospel hymns, and certainly one does not find as many metaphors per hymn in Watts. However, it is possible to approximate the method, and since the conclusions are based on relative proportions, the less numerous metaphors of Watts do not affect the overall conclusions.

In the hymns considered, there are hundreds of different metaphorical expressions which must be categorized in some way in order to make them intelligible. I have found it helpful to follow the suggestion of anthropologist James Fernandez, in his essay "Persuasions and Performances,"[1] that metaphor is "a strategic predication upon an inchoate pronoun (an I, a you, a we, a they) which makes a movement" upon a scale of valuation. That is, every metaphor implies a scale; chosen from a given semantic field, it invokes an implicit range of other possible descriptions.[2] Since the relative valuations within that range are presumed shared by speaker and audience, the object or person described is placed higher or lower on the implied scale, if the rhetorical strategy is successful. Fernandez illustrates by an example of the director of the FBI calling the U.S. Attorney General a jellyfish. The term is intended to invoke a scale ranging from hard or stiff (positive) to soft (negative) although, as Fernandez graphically shows, the scales could be twisted, realigned, or reversed and used for other purposes. Nor are the values always in terms of opposite extremes. One can imagine, for example, a text which exploits the metaphor of "shepherd" to describe Jesus without implying a negative valuation of other conventional metaphorical attributions like "king" or "teacher." Or metaphors like shepherd and king might appear together in such a way as to communicate a paradox. The variety of possibilities is considerable. In order to understand the use of particular metaphors, one must try to discover the character of the field from which it was chosen. Its implications become clearer as one elucidates more and more of the entire system of predications employed in a particular text.

In the hymns, the repetitive and parallel structures provide considerable aid in doing this. Often the hymns are symmetrical, as in the following, where the first and last verses and/or the chorus express a general, recurring theme which subsumes the metaphors used in verses 2 and 3:

When the storms of life are raging,
Tempests wild on sea and land,
I will seek a place of refuge
In the shadow of God's hand.

Though He may send some affliction,
'Twill but make me long for home;
For in love and not in anger,
All his chastenings will come.

Enemies may strive to injure,
Satan all his arts employ;
He will turn what seems to harm me
Into everlasting joy.

So, while here the cross I'm bearing,
Meeting storms and billows wild,
Jesus, for my soul is caring,
Naught can harm His Father's child.

CHORUS:
He will hide me, He will hide me,
Where no harm can e'er betide me;
He will hide me, safely hide me
In the shadow of His hand.

(GH 119)

The first and last verses are elaborations on the metaphors of storm and refuge, the chorus on refuge alone. Verses two and three specify subsets, as it were, of descriptions from different semantic fields, which fall into categories articulating parallel continua of value: afflictions and injury contrasted with home and joy. The verses are analogues to one another, with the first and last plus the chorus providing the hymn with a symmetry and unity and, in this case, an over-all theme. From the point of view of our interest in metaphors and implied scales, we can express it diagrammatically:

1. Storm, tempest ____________ God as refuge (1,Ch)
2. Afflications, chastenings _______ Longing for home
3. Enemies, Satan, harm ____________ Everlasting joy
4. Storms and billows ________________ Jesus caring

Many hymns have a much looser structure, but that kind of parallelism and analogizing occurs frequently enough that it supplies an internal guide to relationships among different sets of metaphors, a key to the parallel continua of value (like the parallel lines above) which are being employed. Journeys in the wilderness may be analogous to storms, to attacks by enemies, to sorrow and woe; and those all contrasted with home, harbor, Jesus as defender, joy, and love. As these examples suggest, and also as indicated in the text proper, there are few if any intermediate steps on the continuum between the two poles; the hymns are sharply dualistic. Nevertheless the general point holds; and the importance of this way of considering the issue would make it possible to account for any cases in which in-between metaphors did arise.

The notion of implied scales of value is important also in order to avoid an overly literal interpretation of metaphors, a temptation too often succumbed to in discussing popular literature with its less complicated structures. The hymns as a whole would be misunderstood if we were to take them as frontal attack on specific conditions in the same way as we might read a social reform tract. The strategy of metaphor is more subtle. While, as I have argued, the hymns spring out of a specific situation, they attempt to grasp and transform it not directly but by a generalizing description, in highly conventional forms. To describe someone as a pilgrim does not refer to a specific situation in the 1850s but to a universal human condition, of which any specific case is merely an illustration, from the hymns' point of view. Whatever correspondences we may find between the hymn metaphors and the actual situations in which they were composed or sung, we must recognize that finding such correspondences does not totally explain the strategy. The hymnists might well respond, after we tell them that the situation of the 1857–58 revival was a response to the threat from the Slave-Power, "But of course, that's just the point: the world is always under the control of evil powers." The hymns' proposed solutions, too, are intended to be *the* answer for all time. That is, they make a claim to ultimacy. Of course, we can say that all this comes down to is that the hymns speak of sin versus salvation and, we might add, in a conversionist form. But there are many ways of conceiving of sin and salvation; so that while those terms are the umbrella terms, so to speak, which cover the ends of the continua of value on which metaphoric predication takes place, there are numerous alternatives of description which can fit within that broad scheme. It is at that point, where the descriptions of sin and salvation in the gospel hymns differ from those in other hymnals, that one can locate their distinctive rhetoric.

In short, what I wish to do is steer a road between a literalist interpretation of metaphors (pilgrim=frontiersman) and one which subsumes them all under Christian doctrine; that is, an interpretive strategy which describes the metaphoric world as a whole system, and only then enters upon an analysis of the situation. Fernandez's notions of continua of value are useful here, and the structure of the hymns themelves supports the use of his approach. From a careful reading of the lyrics, it is possible to infer several classes of metaphorical expression representing different semantic fields and scales of value, some of which are mutually analogous while others are not. For example, sometimes people are described in terms of inner emotions (sorrow, joy, fear), other times in terms of physical condition (weak, strong, sick, whole, lame); in still other portrayals the emphasis is on the total situation, with the person wandering in the wilderness or struggling through the desert. Those clearly represent different semantic fields. Yet in many cases it is evident that they are also analogous descriptions of the "same" situation. One finds them not only in parallel verses, as above, but also in such phrases as "sorrow's rudest tempest" (GH 665.3) and "waves of sorrow roll" (GH 702.2), where metaphors from two different semantic fields are brought together in the same context. Their continua of value are, in Fernandez's phrase, "so melded as to be indistinguishable." Other expressions, like descriptions of people as "guilty" sinners, may appear to us to refer to inward conditions like emotions, but in fact occur in contexts where legal and economic language is employed, and often appear in different hymns than do the other kinds of metaphors. Thus, while one cannot make absolute distinctions, it is generally possible to group distinctive sets of metaphors into classes according to the type of description they employ (for example, inward states, physical conditions, etc.) and in light of their semantic contexts within a hymn. On that basis I have grouped the hymn metaphors into the seven principal classes described in Chapter 1 and listed in Table 2 below, each of which has two opposite poles as endpoints, implying positive or negative values. There are other metaphors which occur rarely, like those of the class "slavery versus freedom," and those which refer in detail to attributes of God; they have been excluded because they occur with a maximum frequency of one or two percent in *Gospel Hymns.* Also excluded are those which appear *only* in *Gospel Hymns* and thus provide no comparative base. Notably, this is the case for premillennial language; where relevant, such topics appear in the table on themes and are discussed in the interpretation in Chapter 2.

Using the seven groupings, I have identified the dominant kinds of metaphors in each hymnal by means of a simple frequency distribution count, noting each time a metaphor of one of those kinds occurred. In cases where a particular metaphor was repeated over and over, as a tag-line to a couplet or in a refrain, I gave it an arbitrary weight of 5—to account for its special reinforcing function without overweighing that particular hymn in which it occurred (where actual and possible repetitions could have been very numerous). The form of verse-and-chorus might seem to pose special problems in this regard, but I think in the case of the hymns considered herein they can be circumvented. The Watts and Wesley hymnals have only verses, no choruses, the refrain having been introduced only in the camp-meeting revivals of early nineteenth-century America. Dickson Bruce, in his book *And They All Sang Hallelujah,* has discussed the significance of that form in relation to the minister-and-audience structure of the revival itself.[3] Later revival hymns, including the gospel hymns, often retained that form. But by the time of the gospel hymns, designed for a literate audience who could read words *and* music, the contrast between the more complex verse and the simpler chorus had diminished, as also had the distinction between minister and laity in the wake of the lay revivals. Therefore it is not necessary to consider the chorus as a separate *kind* of statement, as would be appropriate if it were sung, say, antiphonally. Rather I have simply taken into account its repetitive character (it was sung once for each verse, as well as frequently containing repetitions within itself) and its tendency to be remembered since it often, as James C. Downey has pointed out, condensed the principal thought of the hymn.[4]

It might be argued that the frequency of metaphors does not in itself provide an adequate guide to the content of the hymns, because this microscopic mode of analysis does not yield an overall picture of the impact of the hymn as a whole. That argument is weak for several reasons: (1) often an audience knows and sings only fragments of many hymns, so that it would be difficult to determine which parts represent the hymn as a whole; (2) repetitive structures—those heavily reinforced—occur at the metaphorical level; and (3) the arrangements of metaphors in parallel contrastive pairs is a much stronger structure than the hymn as a whole. Nevertheless I agree in principle that there should be some means of cross-checking the metaphoric analysis, and for that reason I have included the dimension of theme. I have discussed that in the text proper. Some hymns do range over a variety of topics and therefore are difficult to describe in terms of one central theme; those I have left unclassified, but fortunately they are few in number. The distribution of typical themes is recorded in Table 3.

As pointed out in Chapter 2, the dimension of the hymn forms is extremely important. One could of course analyze the general form of popular poetry, but that would be useful only in comparison with other genres, whereas in the case at hand we are looking for distinctive features within one traditional genre. Therefore I have concentrated on the "mode of address" of the hymns, asking to whom the hymn is addressed and what kind of address is made. I have classified the predominant forms as follows:

1. Descriptions; no audience specified
   a. Statements, affirmations
   b. Stories
2. Exhortations to a human audience
   a. To sinners (for example, "come to Jesus!")
   b. To Christians (for example, "work!" "have faith!")
3. Invocations to a deity
   a. Praise and thanksgiving
   b. Supplication, request for help

Although, as in the case of themes, there are instances where the various forms are mixed within a hymn, usually one or another is dominant. When in doubt, I have regarded the chorus as more important than the verses because of its repetitive use, and the first and last verses as more significant than the intervening ones. The relative frequency of each type in each of the hymnals is presented in Table 4.

Some questions might be raised about the value of the quantitative approach to analysis; certainly quantitative analysis of the content of communications had had many proponents and opponents.[5] My survey of the relevant literature suggests that it has been most convincing when applied to materials which are structurally homogeneous and mutually substitutable, as I have suggested is true of the gospel hymns. In my judgment, there is little to quarrel with in Bernard Berelson's classic approach, so far as content itself is concerned. As he points out, in many respects the counting procedure is only making more precise and repeatable what formerly was done impressionistically (compare Kenneth Burke's equation of the "symbolic" with the "statistical" in his *Philosophy of Literary Form*[6]). There is more to be considered, however, than just content; as critics Alexander George, George Gerbner, and Ole Holsti have observed, matters of form and context affect the impact of content itself. For that reason quantitative analysis is useful but must be supplemented by other, more literary methods. In the present study verification comes from consideration of form and from the supplementary materials discussed in Chapters 3–5.

In considering the other hymnals besides *Gospel Hymns,* I have not attemped to insure a scientifically random sample from each hymnal, but have used hymns from each in sufficient numbers which seem also from my reading to be representative of the range of the hymnal as a whole. From the Watts, Hastings and Mason, and Leavitt books I selected fifty each; from the Wesley hymnal, which is much larger and arranged according to divisions of various sizes, I used fifty-five in order to have a 10 percent sample and to include at least one hymn from each division.

TABLE 1
Authorship of *Gospel Hymns*

			Author's sex		Author's nationality			
Date written	Number		Male	Female	Amer.	Brit.	Other	Unknown
pre-1800	99	104	103	1	1	91	8	4
1801–20	5							
1821–40	23	615	418	197	326	121	5	163
1841–60	55							
1861–91	369							
undated	168							

TABLE 2
Relative Frequency of Hymn Metaphors

Type of Metaphor	Watts (%)	Wesley (%)	H&M (%)	Lyre (%)	GH (%)
1. Negative v. positive emotions	16.8	22.7	30.7	17.0	29.3
2. Turmoil v. rest	7.4	13.2	13.0	21.3	21.5
3. Weakness v. strength	3.2	15.3	13.4	10.2	13.5
4. Darkness v. light	2.6	3.5	3.0	6.2	7.1
5. Battle v. victory	12.1	5.6	6.1	8.9	5.2
6. Purity v. impurity	0.0	7.6	1.3	5.2	3.8
7. Guilt v. atonement	57.8	32.2	32.5	31.1	19.5

NOTE: Due to rounding, percentages do not always total 100%.

TABLE 3
Relative Frequency of Hymn Themes

Theme	Watts (%)	Wesley (%)	H&M (%)	Lyre (%)	GH (%)
God: creator, holy, powerful	20	9.1	10	8	0.5
God/Jesus: conqueror-king	6	3.6	2	0	1.0
Repentance, atonement, damnation; Jesus a mediator	38	16.3	24	24	3.8
Grace, salvation	4	18.2	12	10	15.8
Jesus: refuge, guide, helper	8	9.1	16	14	14.8
Jesus: healer	0	3.6	8	6	1.1
Jesus: loving and beloved	8	14.5	8	10	17.4
Heaven	4	1.8	2	2	15.6
Christian pilgrimage	0	1.8	0	4	4.2
Mission, service	2	1.8	4	2	6.7
Christian fellowship and joy	2	1.8	4	4	0.2
Battle, storm	2	1.8	2	6	5.7
Jesus: suffering	2	1.8	4	2	2.0
Jesus: light and beauty	0	1.8	2	0	.3
Holy Spirit, revival	0	1.8	0	0	1.5
Vanity of world	2	0.0	0	4	0.0
Purity	0	5.5	0	2	2.1
Miscellaneous: Sabbath, Bible, morality, home, patriotism	2	0.0	0	2	2.1
Unclassified	0	5.5	0	0	5.5

NOTE: Due to rounding, percentages do not always total 100%.

TABLE 4
Relative Frequency of Hymn Forms

Form	Watts (%)	Wesley (%)	H&M (%)	Lyre (%)	GH (%)
1. Descriptions					
a. Statements, affirmations	36	16.4	20	34	38.2
b. Stories	0	0.0	4	12	13.3
TOTAL	36	16.4	24	46	51.5
2. Exhortations					
a. To sinners	4	3.6	22	10	14.5
b. To Christians	0	1.8	2	2	11.2
TOTAL	4	5.4	24	12	25.7
3. Invocations					
a. Praise and thanksgiving	42	21.8	26	20	8.5
b. Supplication, request	18	56.4	26	22	14.3
TOTAL	60	78.2	52	42	22.8

Notes

Chapter 1
The Gospel Hymns of Moody and Sankey: A Problem in Rhetorical Criticism

1. *New York Times,* June 22, 1875, p. 6, col. 1. The full quotation: "The Moody and Sankey fever in England has been a mystery to everybody on this side the Atlantic, and can only be accounted for on the theory of the gravedigger in 'Hamlet,' that in England everybody is mad."

2. "Singing the gospel" was a phrase popularized by Philip Phillips, and often used by Sankey and others afterwards; see George C. Stebbins, *Reminiscences and Gospel Hymn Stories* (New York: George H. Doran Co., 1924; rpt. New York: AMS Press, 1971), p. 141, and Ira D. Sankey, *Sankey's Story of the Gospel Hymns and of Sacred Songs and Solos* (Philadelphia: Sunday School Times Co., 1906), p. 198. After Moody's death in 1899, Sankey occasionally gave lectures under the title, "Sacred Song and Story" (p. 150).

The rubric "gospel hymns" goes back to 1836, when Edward Mote published his *System of Praise, A New Selection of Gospel Hymns,* according to Fred Daniel Gealy in *Companion to the Hymnal: A Handbook to the 1964 Methodist Hymnal* (Nashville: Abingdon Press, 1970), p. 624; on the other hand, Rubert Murrell Stevenson, in "Ira D. Sankey and 'Gospel Hymnody,' " *Religion in Life* 20 (1950–51): 85, attributes it to Sankey.

William G. McLoughlin, Jr., in his *Modern Revivalism: Charles Grandison Finney to Billy Graham* (New York: Ronald Press, 1959), holds that it was Moody who made Sankey famous, and that people were just as enthralled by Moody's sermons as by Sankey's singing. Contemporary testimony is fairly evenly divided on the relative impact of the two men, but it is equally clear that the hymns had a longer life and were used in wider circles than Moody's printed sermons.

3. For accounts of the tours, see, for example, E. J. Goodspeed, *The Wonderful Career of Moody and Sankey in Great Britain and America* (New

York: Henry Goodspeed, 1876); John Hall and George H. Stuart, *The American Evangelists, D. L. Moody and Ira D. Sankey, in Great Britain and Ireland* (New York: Dodd & Mead, 1875); Elias Nason, *American Evangelists: An Account of Their Work in England and America* (Boston: Lathrop & Co., 1877); John Macpherson, *Revival and Revival-work: An Account of the Labours of D. L. Moody, Ira D. Sankey, and Other Evangelists* (London: Morgan and Scott, 1878); and Rufus Clark, *The Work of God in Great Britain: Under Mssrs. Moody and Sankey, 1873 to 1875* (New York: Harper & Brothers, 1875). See also the Moody biographies; the two most recent are J. C. Pollock, *Moody: A Biographical Portrait of the Pacesetter in Modern Mass Evangelism* (New York: Macmillan Co., 1963), and James F. Findlay, Jr., *Dwight L. Moody: American Evangelist, 1837–1899* (Chicago: University of Chicago Press, 1969), the latter being the best and most thorough biographical treatment. Accounts within the context of the historiography of revivalism include McLoughlin, *Modern Revivalism,* and Bernard A. Weisberger, *They Gathered at the River* (Chicago: Quadrangle Books, 1958).

4. W. R. Moody, *The Life of Dwight L. Moody* (New York: Fleming H. Revell Co., 1900), p. 186; Stevenson, "Sankey and 'Gospel Hymnody,' " p. 84.

5. Louis F. Benson, *The English Hymn: Its Development and Use in Worship* (New York: Hodder & Stoughton, 1915), p. 485. There had been spurts of revival activity in England since about 1858 which had encouraged the development of hymnody, and mass evangelical services over a period of months were known from 1851 and 1855; see William Jensen Reynolds, *A Survey of Christian Hymnody* (New York: Holt, Rinehart & Winston, 1963), pp. 105–6, and Horton Davies, *Worship and Theology in England* (5 vols.; Princeton, N.J.: Princeton University Press, 1961–75), 4:86.

6. That figure, from the *Ira D. Sankey Centenary* (New Castle, Pa.: n.p., 1941), p. 35, may be an exaggeration; but with no publishers' accounts available, it is difficult to judge. Certainly the sales were extraordinary. Sankey himself says with some lack of modesty that the collection sold more than any book except the Bible (*Story,* p. 20). Henry Wilder Foote, in *Three Centuries of American Hymnody* (Cambridge: Harvard University Press, 1940), states that Sankey's books sold fifty million copies (p. 267), but he does not specify whether that figure includes both American and English editions, or only one or the other. Robert G. McCutchan, *Hymns in the Lives of Men* (New York: Abingdon-Cokesbury Press, 1945), p. 169, gives the same figure for the American compilations by Sankey. John Julian, writing closest in

time to Sankey in the article on him in *A Dictionary of Hymnology* (rev. ed.; London: J. Murray, 1908), makes no guess; like Benson, he is content simply to record the enormity of the books' popularity. Benson does point out that the first issues of *Sacred Songs and Solos,* which sold at first for sixpence a copy, brought Moody and Sankey, while they were still touring Britain, royalties of £7000 (*English Hymn,* pp. 486–87)! Further, when one considers that far lesser personages in the States were selling Sunday-school hymnals in editions of 100,000 to 500,000 copies, the grandiose claims for sales in the tens of millions seem easier to believe. (For the latter figures, see Jacob Henry Hall, *Biography of Gospel Song and Hymn Writers* [New York: Fleming H. Revell Co., 1914; rpt. New York: AMS Press, 1971], and Gealy, *Companion,* p. 495.)

7. Sankey, *Story,* p. 20; Benson, *English Hymn,* pp. 485–87; Reynolds, *Survey,* pp. 105–6; David R. Breed, *The History and Use of Hymns and Hymn-Tunes* (New York: Fleming H. Revell Co., 1902), pp. 331–33.

8. Benson, *English Hymn,* p. 487; Edwin H. Pierce, " 'Gospel Hymns' and Their Tunes," *Musical Quarterly* 26 (1940): 356.

9. H. Wiley Hitchcock, Introduction to the 1972 reprint of the Excelsior Edition. Full title is *Gospel Hymns Nos. 1 to 6 Complete,* by Ira D. Sankey, James McGranahan, and George C. Stebbins (New York: Biglow & Main Co.; Cincinnati: John Church Co., 1895; rpt. New York: Da Capo Press, 1972). All references henceforth to *Gospel Hymns* signify this work in the 1972 facsimile reprint. The various numbers of the series appeared in 1875, 1876, 1878, 1881, 1887, and 1891, with the cumulative edition of numbers 1 through 4 coming out in 1886.

10. Reynolds, *Survey,* p. 106.

11. Originally the Sunday-school teacher was also an itinerant seller of music books, which he often compiled himself when his classes had need for new materials. This created a new profession, that of music teacher, with income from both teaching and the sale of his collections. See Hamilton Crawford Macdougall, *Early New England Psalmody: An Historical Appreciation, 1620–1820* (Brattleboro, Vt.: Stephen Daye Press, 1940), p. 100.

12. For some discussion of these figures, see George Frederick Root, *The Story of a Musical Life* (Cincinnati: John Church Co., 1891), and Dena Epstein, *Music Publishing in Chicago before 1871: The Firm of Root & Cady* (Detroit: Information Coordinators, 1969).

13. Besides Bliss, Sankey, Stebbins, McGranahan and those named

above, there were Philip Phillips, Hubert P. Main, William G. Fischer, T. C. O'Kane, H. R. Palmer, and C. C. Case. For some of the interrelationships among the musicians and leading evangelists, see Stebbins, *Reminiscences,* pp. 45–48, 71–75, and D. W. Whittle, *A Memoir of P. P. Bliss* (New York: A. S. Barnes & Co., 1877).

14. Bradbury had collaborated with Hastings and Mason; Sherwin had been Mason's student; Root had worked with him in the early Normal Institutes which Mason had set up for training music teachers. See Foote, *Three Centuries,* p. 264, and the article on Sherwin in Julian, *Dictionary*; also Root, *Musical Life,* chs. 2–5. For a brief discussion of their musical debt to Mason, see H. Wiley Hitchcock, *Music in the United States: A Historical Introduction* (Englewood Cliffs, N.J.: Prentice-Hall, 1969), p. 100. He notes that the gospel-hymn writers added the resounding refrain known from camp-meeting hymns earlier in the century.

15. All the basic histories of hymnody trace this development; see especially Benson, *English Hymn,* pp. 292–98, and Foote, *Three Centuries,* pp. 166–86; also Gilbert Chase, *America's Music: From the Pilgrims to the Present* (New York: McGraw-Hill Book Co., 1955), pp. 183–231. For a treatment of the frontier camp-meeting hymns, see Dickson Bruce, *And They All Sang Hallelujah: Plain-Folk Camp-Meeting Religion, 1800–1845* (Knoxville: University of Tennessee Press, 1974). I will not deal with the other strands of revival tradition, notably among Southern blacks, which also developed a "gospel hymn" form.

16. Although there will not be space to make the argument herein, I would suggest that the branch of revivalism represented by Sankey's gospel hymns has affinities, morphologically speaking, with "devotional" or "pietistic" traditions in other cultural settings, even outside Western culture. Revivalism's focus on an intimate relationship with one deity, its strong accent on the pleasures of an afterlife in a paradise ruled by the deity, its departure from traditional religious structures of organization and leadership, its use of popular media—all those characteristics are shared by certain *bhakti* movements in India and Amidist (Pure Land Buddhist) groups in Japan. One can find movements with varying degrees of similarity in other traditions.

Treatments of devotionalism by historians of religions have, however, been few and far between. For some discusions in a comparative framework, see G. van der Leeuw, *Religion in Essence and Manifestation,* trans. J. E. Turner (2 vols., 1938; rpt. New York: Harper & Row, 1963), 2:510–11, 613–16; Rudolf Otto, *Christianity and the Indian Religion of Grace,* trans. H. Bjerrum (Madras: Christian Literature Society for India, 1929); Friedrich Heiler, *Erscheinungsformen und Wesen der Religion* (Stuttgart: W. Kohlhammer, 1961), pp. 529, 546–47; Nathan Söderblom, *The Living God: Basal Forms of Personal Religion* (London: Oxford University Press, 1933), chs. 4–5. Edward C. Dimock, Jr., has suggested another sort of avenue to comparison in his brief discussion of the "logics" of Vaiṣṇava and Sahajiyā poetry and doctrine, compared to medieval Christian poetry and doctrine; see his *The Place of the Hidden Moon* (Chicago: University of Chicago Press, 1966), ch. 1.

17. McLoughlin, *Modern Revivalism,* pp. 6–11. According to his interpretation, there have been four major awakenings in America: 1725–50, 1795–1835, 1875–1915, and 1945–?, each of which coincided with a cultural crisis and a general reorientation. His formulation is on the one hand so general that it can account for anything, and amounts to little more than a statement of the form "social change produces religious change," without specifying what constitutes significant change in either case. On the other hand, the very generality of his explanatory framework allows him to fill in the gaps with any number of "critical" events—sometimes war, sometimes depression, sometimes dissatisfaction with the churches—which can serve as causes of revivals. For a more specific critique and my proposed alternative, see Chapter 6.

18. I am indebted to my colleague in musicology, David Young, for this observation.

19. See, for example, Asa Hull's instructions on the teaching of music to children, in the preface to his *The Gem of Gems: A Choice Collection of Sacred Songs* (New York: Daniel W. Knowles; Chicago: Henry A. Sumner & Company, 1881); and Henry C. Fish, *Handbook of Revivals: For the Use of Winners of Souls* (Boston: James H. Earle, 1874), pp. 318–19. Sankey especially was known for his emphasis on singing the message carefully, even at the expense of musical requirements; see Edward F. Rimbault, "A Few Words on the Music of Messrs. Moody and Sankey," *Leisure Hour* (London) 34 (1875): 476. Rimbault, a music critic, believed that the words had "a great deal to do with the popularity of the tunes" (p. 475). That is supported by what is known of Lowell Mason's style of music instruction, as described by H. Crosby Englizian in his *Brimstone Corner: Park Street Church, Boston* (Chicago: Moody Press, 1968), p. 118.

20. Geertz's "Religion as a Cultural System," originally published in 1965, is readily accessible in the *Reader in Comparative Religion: An Anthropological Approach,* ed. William A. Lessa and Evon Z. Vogt (3rd ed.; New York: Harper & Row, 1972). His definition of symbol in this

essay is taken from Susanne Langer, *Philosophy in a New Key* (New York: New American Library, 1942).

21. *The Interpretation of Cultures* (New York: Basic Books, 1973). Comments on the interpretive process are found also in "Deep Play," which I have cited from *Myth, Symbol, and Culture,* ed. Clifford Geertz (New York: W. W. Norton & Co., 1971).

22. Geertz, *Islam Observed* (Chicago: University of Chicago Press, 1968).

23. For his comments on theory, see "Deep Play," p. 29. Examples of broad concepts he thinks are useful are " 'integration, 'rationalization,' 'symbol,' 'ideology,' 'ethos,' 'revolution,' 'identity,' 'metaphor,' 'structure,' 'ritual,' 'world view,' 'actor,' 'function,' 'sacred,' and, of course, 'culture' itself." For Geertz, these are theoretical because they constitute a "repertoire" of concepts "woven into the body of thick-description ethnography in the hope of rendering mere occurrences scientifically eloquent" ("Thick Description," p. 28). This is, however, hardly adequate for a theory. Geertz does undertake comparison in his *Islam Observed* and discusses there his notion of "the religious perspective" in general terms; but his descriptions of Islam in Morocco and Indonesia serve primarily to contrast the styles of the two cultures. Further, his comparisons and contrasts clearly rest on a typology of charismatic authority appropriated from Weber—which he acknowledges in passing but which informs his description more than he seems inclined to admit.

24. Beginning with the *Elementary Structures of Kinship,* trans. J. H. Bell, J. R. von Sturmer, and Rodney Needham, ed. (rev. ed.; Boston: Beacon Press, 1969; Fr. orig. 1949) and especially *The Savage Mind* (Chicago: University of Chicago Press, 1966; Fr. orig. 1962), the works of Lévi-Strauss have provided impetus for studies in "cognitive anthropology," especially studies of systems of classification. The tradition goes back further, to the essay by Émile Durkheim and Marcel Mauss, *Primitive Classification,* trans. and ed. Rodney Needham (Chicago: University of Chicago Press, 1963; orig. in *Année sociologique,* vol. 6 [1901–2]). For a review of some studies in cognitive anthropology, see William Sturtevant, "Studies in Ethnoscience," *American Anthropologist* 66 (1964): 99–131. For examples, consult Charles Frake, "The Ethnographic Study of Cognitive Systems," in *Theory in Anthropology,* ed. Robert A. Manners and David Kaplan (Chicago: Aldine Publishing Company, 1968); and sec. 4 in Lessa and Vogt, eds., *Reader,* entitled "Symbolic Classification."

25. Peter Berger and Thomas Luckmann, *The Social Construction of*

Reality: A Treatise in the Sociology of Knowledge (Garden City, N.Y.: Doubleday & Co., 1966). That work builds largely upon that of phenomenologist and sociologist Alfred Schutz, working on the foundations of Edmund Husserl and Max Weber. See especially Luckmann's jointly authored edition of his later work: Thomas Luckmann and Alfred Schutz, *The Structures of the Life-World* (Evanston, Ill.: Northwestern University Press, 1973). This is a parallel tradition, so to speak, in attempting to lay a foundation for studying cognitive structures in society; but to my knowledge it has not been developed further toward the study of language, as has happened in structuralism.

26. For an example of Lévi-Strauss's method, see "The Structural Study of Myth," in *Structural Anthropology,* trans. C. Jacobson and B. G. Schoepf (Garden City, N.Y.: Doubleday & Co., 1963; Fr. orig. 1958), 1: 225–26; the study of myth has been elaborated in his four-volume *Mythologiques* (Paris: Librairie Plon, 1964–72).

Geertz has sharply criticized the cognitive anthropologists on several grounds. He has attacked them for adopting a "privacy theory of meaning" which sees culture as made up of "mental phenomena" ("Thick Description," pp. 10–13). This is a strange charge to level against the heirs of Durkheim and Mauss, but there have been some unfortunate formulations among the cognitive anthropologists (and indeed in Durkheim) which seem to relegate culture to an undefined mental realm, and which have given rise to futile debates over whether the categories that "we" (the ethnographers) devise really exist in "their" (the informants') heads. (See, for example, Robbins Burling, "Cognition and Componential Analysis: God's Truth or Hocus-Pocus?" *American Anthropologist* 66 [1964]: 20–28, and Anthony F. C. Wallace, "The Psychic Unity of Human Groups," in *Theory in Anthropology,* ed. Manners and Kaplan.) More relevant to our discussion is Geertz's opposition to the tendency of some "cognitive anthropologists" to reduce complex systems to a simple set of dichotomies and their elaborations. In a passage which seems to be directed against Lévi-Strauss, Geertz writes: "To set forth symmetrical crystals of significance, purified of the material complexity in which they were located, and then attribute their existence to autogenous principles of order, universal properties of the human mind, or vast, a priori *weltanschauungen,* is to pretend a science that does not exist and imagine a reality that cannot be found. Cultural analysis is (or should be) guessing at meanings, assessing the guesses, and drawing explanatory conclusions from the better guesses, not discovering the Continent of Meaning and mapping out its bodiless landscape" ("Thick Description," p. 20). By converting culture into rules, into a series of eternally repeated oppositions and mediations, one loses what makes it interesting. I would agree with that judgment; and yet when one is engaged in making "guesses," constructing hypotheses, structural analysis of texts can be a useful starting point. And while, clearly, Geertz is on the side of the angels when he insists that we should look at texts, at practice, at activity—whether in gesture or ritual or literature—that does not mean that systematization is not useful.

27. Readers familiar with current anthropological theory might wonder why I do not take up the work of Mary Douglas, who has offered in *Natural Symbols* (rev. ed.; Baltimore: Penguin Books, 1973) a provocative theory designed to show relationships between cosmology and social situation. Of course, she does not deal with the problem of "texts," but only with features of the belief systems of groups. I consider that an important weakness, but nevertheless I would be remiss if I did not mention her work here.

Douglas has outlined her theory of types of societies in terms of two variables, "grid" and "group." Since *Natural Symbols,* she has modified her description, in the Frazer Lecture for 1976, "Cosmology," which is unpublished at the time of this writing, and on which I will rely here. "Group" measures social pressure along a continuum from that placed on the individual who spends time with and interacts with people in multiple groups (in the extreme case belonging to no group), to the person who identifies totally with one group which provides the framework of all his associations and in terms of which he justifies all his behavior. Grid defines the range of social role-definitions, from a situation in which roles are loose and ambiguous, permitting individual autonomy and free transactions, to one in which the role is carefully and unambiguously defined by the society and insulation from transactions with others is maximal. The intersection of these dimensions provides us with four ideal-types of societies, which may best be described by example. At low-grid/weak-group one finds modern capitalist society, composed of freely transacting individuals in competition. At low-grid/strong-group is the small sect with sharp boundaries between inside and outside but little internal differentiation. The classic case of high-grid/strong-group would be a hierarchically organized society like medieval Europe, while an example of high-grid/weak-group would be plantation slavery, where roles are carefully defined but the individual has no group membership in that there is no one with whom he is permitted to interact effectively. Each type of society produces its own distinctive cosmology (except in the fourth case where there is, Douglas says, little theoretical elaboration of any kind), including attitudes toward time, space, nature, society, and a variety of other issues.

Douglas's theory turns out to be difficult to apply when dealing with a pluralistic society like the nineteenth-century urban North because the force of various group memberships and role definitions is difficult to chart. Perhaps for this reason, Douglas in her latest formulation has insisted that group be defined in terms of social pressures deriving from face-to-face contact. But this in turn makes it nearly impossible to employ the theory in historical investigation where the relevant contacts remain obscure; and certainly when we are dealing with mass popular literature as in the gospel hymns, other factors besides intimate group interaction are at work.

More importantly, I am not convinced that the variables of grid and group are independent as is required by her theory. Increase in the number of groups to which a person belongs (a move from strong to weak group) would seem to imply a proliferation of possible roles, a diminishing of the stringency with which roles are defined, and less insulation (a move from high to low grid). I suspect that the theory is best understood as a schematization of the force of identities people adopt—the extent to which they understand themselves to be fulfilling a role or station (such as an occupation), or to be primarily a member of a group (an Israelite, a socialist, or whatever). These are extremely important features of society, and Douglas must be appreciated for emphasizing and attempting to systematize them. Her ideal types may thus serve as a useful starting point. But I have found a similar kind of framework implied in Burke's concept of "identification," discussed below; and this is a more flexible one which may be more useful in historical contexts where first-hand observation is not possible. I do discuss in note 8 to Chapter 4 how I think my material fits into Douglas's theory and how it raises questions about it.

28. Among Burke's works, see especially *Philosophy of Literary Form* (Baton Rouge: Louisiana State University Press, 1941); *A Rhetoric of Motives* (Englewood Cliffs, N.J.: Prentice-Hall, 1950; rpt. Berkeley and Los Angeles: University of California Press, 1969); *The Rhetoric of Religion: Studies in Logology* (Boston: Beacon Press, 1961); and *Language as Symbolic Action: Essays on Life, Literature, and Method* (Berkeley and Los Angeles: University of California Press, 1966). The term "rhetoric" can be used to refer either to the form of discourse under study, as in Burke's phrase "the rhetoric of religion," or to the activity of the discipline which studies those forms. I use "rhetoric" for the former, "rhetorical criticism" for the latter.

29. Burke calls the three dimensions the "symbolic," the "grammar," and the "rhetoric"; see *Rhetoric of Motives,* pp. 21–23, and "Rhetoric and Poetics," in *Language as Symbolic Action,* pp. 295–303. James L. Peacock, an anthropologist, has criticized views of society as either functional or logical, and has proposed instead a dramatistic view influenced by Burke; see his "Society as Narrative," in *Forms of Symbolic Action: Proceedings of the 1969 Annual Spring Meeting of the American Ethnological Society,* ed. Robert F. Spencer (Seattle: University of Washington Press, 1969).

30. Burke, *Philosophy of Literary Form,* pp. 1, 293–98.

31. For examples of this kind of criticism, see Burke's analysis of the language of Augustine's *Confessions* in *Rhetoric of Religion,* and his interpretations of Shakespeare in *Language as Symbolic Action.*

32. Burke, *Philosophy of Literary Form,* pp. 20, 297; cf. *Language as Symbolic Action,* p. 301.

33. Burke, *Rhetoric of Motives,* pp. 19–31, 35–37; *Language as Symbolic Action,* ch. 1.

34. Mary Douglas comes close to this formulation when, in her Frazer Lecture on "Cosmology," she says that "the operative level of analysis is that at which excuses are required from individuals and made by them and where moral judgements materialize into pressures from other persons to act in certain ways," that is, the level "at which people find it necessary to explain to each other why they behave as they do" (p. 18). Justification is, I think, the other side of persuasion.

For examples of anthropological work which have employed notions of rhetoric in the way suggested by Burke, see James W. Fernandez, "Unbelievably Subtle Words: Representation and Integration in the Sermons of an African Reformative Cult," *History of Religions* 6 (1966): 43–69, and his "Persuasions and Performances: Of the Beast in Every Body . . . and the Metaphors of Everyman," in *Myth, Symbol, and Culture,* ed. Geertz; and James L. Peacock, *Rites of Modernization: Symbolic and Social Aspects of Indonesian Proletarian Drama* (Chicago: University of Chicago Press, 1968). Victor Turner, in his recent *Dramas, Fields, and Metaphors: Symbolic Action in Human Society* (Ithaca, N.Y.: Cornell University Press, 1974), has called his approach "dramatistic" and subtitled the book "symbolic action," but he does not refer to Burke as source of those concepts. His approach has many interesting features, however; and see also his *The Ritual Process: Structure and Anti-Structure* (Chicago: Aldine Publishing Company, 1969), for a clear explication of his basic perspective with some appropriation of structuralist ideas.

Chapter 2
Passivity and Passion: The Strategy of the Gospel Hymns

1. Ira D. Sankey, James McGranahan, and George C. Stebbins, *Gospel Hymns Nos. 1 to 6 Complete* (New York: Biglow & Main Co.; Cincinnati: John Church Co., 1895; rpt. New York: Da Capo Press, 1972), p. 2.

2. For example, *Gospel Hymns* includes, out of its total of 739 hymns, 19 lyrics from Watts and 10 from Charles Wesley. Approximately 5 percent of its hymns had appeared in Thomas Hastings and Lowell Mason's *Spiritual Songs for Social Worship* (Utica, N.Y.: Hastings & Tracy & W. Williams, 1832).

3. For discussions of the history and use of psalmody, see Louis F. Benson, *The English Hymn: Its Development and Use in Worship* (New York: Hodder & Stoughton, 1915); Horton Davies, *The Worship of the English Puritans* (Westminster: Dacre Press; Glasgow: University Press, 1948), and his recently completed study *Worship and Theology in England* (5 vols.; Princeton, N.J.: Princeton University Press, 1961–75); Henry Wilder Foote, "An Account of the Bay Psalm Book," *Hymn Society Papers* 7 (1940): 1–17, and *Three Centuries of American Hymnody,* (Cambridge: Harvard University Press, 1940); Hamilton Crawford Macdougall, *Early New England Psalmody: An Historical Appreciation, 1620–1820* (Brattleboro, Vt.: Stephen Daye Press, 1940); and Helen Rawson Cook, "The Bay Psalm Book and Its Setting" (M.S.M. thesis, Union Theological Seminary, 1941).

Watts's hymns were designed to be correlated with sermon topics, as the indices clearly show. He was undertaking a revision of worship and designing a new "System of Praise" which would eliminate what he regarded as the "Jewishness" of the Puritan psalter and recover the "gospel truth" within it. Thus his changes in the psalmody were supposed to represent what David would have said if he has been a Christian, as suggested by the title: *The Psalms of David Imitated in the Language of the New Testament.* With newly revised psalms and some of his own hymns, the new system could be put into execution. For a discussion of Watts's plans, see Harry Escott, *Isaac Watts, Hymnographer* (London: Independent Press, 1962), pp. 113–60, 192–93. My references to Watts are from the 1819 edition published in London by Alex Muirhead & Co., with the two parts to the "system" bound in one volume.

John Wesley expressly noted the plan of order to his collection in the preface: "The hymns are not carelessly jumbled together, but carefully ranged under proper heads, according to the experience of real

Christians. So that this book is, in effect, a little body of experimental and practical divinity. . . . I would recommend it to every truly pious reader, as a means of raising or quickening the spirit of devotion; of confirming his faith; of enlivening his hope; and of kindling and increasing his love to God and man." The quotation is from the 1877 edition published in London by the Wesleyan Conference Office, pp. iv–v. Sample headings of the types of Christian experience used to classify the hymns: "Exhorting Sinners to Return to God"; "Describing, 1. The Pleasantness of Religion," "2. The Goodness of God"; "Praying for Repentance," "For Mourners Convicted of Sin": "For Believers Rejoicing," "Fighting," "Praying," "Watching"; "For the Society Meeting," "Giving Thanks." See Benson, *English Hymn,* pp. 248–49, and Davies, *Worship and Theology* 3:202, for comments on this aspect of Wesley's hymnal.

4. Frances Jane Crosby Van Alstyne, *Memories of Eighty Years: The Story of Her Life, Told by Herself* (Boston: James H. Earle & Co., 1906), p. 169. Often she wrote under pseudonyms; for a list of the most common ones, see p. 170. Biglow & Main contracted for most of her hymns, and there were records of their having paid her for 5,900 of them (see *Fanny Crosby's Story of Ninety-four Years,* retold by S. Trevena Jackson [New York: Fleming H. Revell Co., 1915], p. 82). On hymns written at the composer's request, see George C. Stebbins, *Reminiscences and Gospel Hymn Stories* (New York: George H. Doran Co., 1924; rpt. New York: AMS Press, 1971), p. 77.

5. On the composers' borrowings from older hymnals, periodicals, and the like, see Stebbins, *Reminiscences,* pp. 82–83, 123, 164–65, and Ira D. Sankey, *Sankey's Story of the Gospel Hymns and of Sacred Songs and Solos* (Philadelphia: Sunday School Times Co., 1906), p. 220. Sometimes, but we do not know how often, compilers paid authors for their verses; reference to this practice appears in Stebbins, *Reminiscences,* pp. 119–20, and Jacob Henry Hall, *Biography of Gospel Song and Hymn Writers* (New York: Fleming H. Revell Co., 1914; rpt. New York: AMS Press, 1971), pp. 174, 252, 257. The latter gives rates of $2.50, $3.00, and $6.25 in different instances. It may be that some who contributed verses were paid as they might have been for contributions to a literary magazine; but most probably volunteered their work, regarding it as sufficient reward to have it accepted and used by a leading evangelist (for an example, see Stebbins, *Reminiscences,* p. 84).

6. See Bruce Bugbee, *Genesis of American Patent and Copyright Law* (Washington, D.C.: Public Affairs Press, 1967), for the history of the laws, and James Appleton Morgan, *The Law of Literature* (2 vols.; New

York: James Cockcroft & Co., 1875), 2:382, for an exposition of the laws relevant at the time. Of course Biglow & Main, having access to William Bradbury's rights on his numerous Sunday-school songbooks, had a considerable mine of material without worrying about a copyright. The Sunday-school books in general were undoubtedly a leading source for the gospel hymns, as suggested in E. J. Goodspeed, *The Wonderful Career of Moody and Sankey in Great Britain and America* (New York: Henry Goodspeed, 1876), p. 242; cf. Robert G. McCutchan, *Hymns in the Lives of Men* (New York: Abingdon-Cokesbury Press, 1945), p. 168.

7. For a breakdown of the authorship, see Table 1, Appendix.

8. It is not possible to date all the hymns precisely, but for the majority one can establish approximate dates by reference to the author's life span and what is known of his or her work. The best source is John Julian's *Dictionary of Hymnology* (rev. ed.; London: J. Murray, 1908), though he is occasionally wrong by a year or two on specific hymns. His material is most deficient with regard to the latter third of the nineteenth century and to American authors; thus it is most likely that the authorship of hymns identified as "unknown" was relatively late in the century and probably American. That is the case for hymns not mentioned by Julian which I have traced through other sources.

9. For the sake of convenient and brief reference to the hymnals, I have devised the following notation for quotations from hymns here and henceforth: in parentheses after the quotation will appear abbreviated hymnal titles or authors: Watts, Wesley, H&M, Lyre, GH. Then will follow the hymn number and, when less than a whole hymn is quoted, a decimal point followed by the verse number and/or by "Ch" for the chorus. Thus GH 628.1 means *Gospel Hymns,* number 628, verse 1.

10. Book I is composed of scriptural paraphrases; Book III is hymns for the Lord's Supper; Book II includes Watts's original lyrics.

11. Wesley's hymns were especially designed for the guiding of spiritual experience through the "bands" and "classes" of devotees. For a good account of those societies, see Frank Baker, *John Wesley and the Church of England* (London: Epworth Press, 1970), pp. 74–79.

12. As Jonathan Z. Smith has pointed out to me, the "worm" was well known to Watts and his successors as the "worm," that is, serpent, in texts such as Milton *Paradise Lost,* ix.1068.

13. That song was not explicitly religious, but was a real tearjerker and one of the most popular of Sankey's selections. It is now preserved for posterity at Disneyland (California), where a barbershop

quartet of assorted animated fowl sings a few lines from the song in the "America's Music" attraction. At the other end of the scale of cultural influence, it should be noted that some of the gospel hymn tunes appear as motifs in the work of composer Charles Ives (for example, Robert Lowry's "Shall We Gather at the River?").

14. Grammar corresponding to content is by no means limited to this example. Samples taken from hymns of uses of verbs and verb forms, and compared with a sample of nineteenth-century prose in a novel (Harriet Beecher Stowe's *Uncle Tom's Cabin*), show the hymns' marked emphasis on passive and intransitive verb forms, as well as on the use of transitive verbs which perform no change in their object (seeing, remembering, etc.—these are mentioned below). For an interesting essay which suggests ways of interpreting such data, see M. A. K. Halliday, "The Syntax Enunciates the Theme," in *Rules and Meanings,* ed. Mary Douglas (Baltimore: Penguin Books, 1973). Here it can only be briefly suggested that the verb forms in general may support the emphasis on passivity and rest.

15. Sherman, the story goes, waved a white signal flag tied to a pine tree from the top of Kenesaw Mountain in Georgia; seen by a beleaguered contingent at Altoona Pass twenty miles away, it gave the men courage to fight on against overwhelming odds. Sankey reports that Sherman's pine tree was cut down a few years after the war and was fashioned into souvenirs—from among which he himself received a conductor's baton (*Story,* pp. 100–102).

16. The nature of the missionary enterprise differed in Britain and America, of course, but the ideology of it shows the same contours as far as the hymns are concerned.

17. Davies, *Worship and Theology,* 3:34.

18. Moody uses that very analogy in one of his stories, speaking of what a preacher or teacher of the gospel must do. See Dwight L. Moody, *Anecdotes and Illustrations of D. L. Moody,* comp. J. B. McClure (Chicago: Rhodes & McClure, 1878), pp. 37–38.

Chapter 3
Passion and Order: The Problem of Social Religion

1. Such practices were common in the earlier camp meetings as well, but it was with the Finney revivals that discussion of them became prominent in the literature. For historical accounts of those revivals, see William G. McLoughlin, Jr., *Modern Revivalism: Charles Grandison Finney to Billy Graham* (New York: Ronald Press, 1959), Bernard A.

Weisberger, *They Gathered at the River* (Chicago: Quadrangle Books, 1958), and Whitney R. Cross, *The Burned-Over District: The Social and Intellectual History of Enthusiastic Religion in Western New York, 1800–1850* (Ithaca, N.Y.: Cornell University Press, 1950; rpt. New York: Harper & Row, 1961).

2. The minutes were printed in the *New York Observer* and then reprinted, with an appropriately derogatory introduction, as "Dr. Beecher and Mr. Beman's Convention on Revivals," in the Unitarian journal *Christian Examiner and Theological Review* 4 (1827): 357–70; my quotations are from the latter. As Leonard Sweet has observed in "The View of Man Inherent in New Measures Revivalism," *Church History* 45 (1976): 206–21, many of the "new measures" were not new except in intensity and style (see esp. pp. 211–12 and note 39). Even on the matter of social prayer, one can find precursors, for example, in Jonathan Edwards's idea of the "concert of prayer," mentioned in his *An Humble Attempt to Promote . . . Visible Union,* quoted in Alan Heimert and Perry Miller, eds., *The Great Awakening* (Indianapolis: Bobbs-Merrill, 1967), pp. 569–70.

3. "Convention," pp. 358, 360.

4. Ibid., p. 362. The objection probably refers to lay exhortation as well as to narration of personal experience; as Charles G. Finney noted, the question of lay exhortation had "agitated all New England" (*Lectures on Revivals of Religion,* ed. William G. McLoughlin, Jr., John Harvard Library [Cambridge: Harvard University Press, 1960], p. 258). Finney's *Lectures,* a classic of the period, were originally delivered to his New York congregation and transcribed by Joshua Leavitt, editor of the *New York Evangelist* (whom we have already met as compiler of *The Christian Lyre*), and published therein in 1835. McLoughlin's introduction to the John Harvard Library edition provides an excellent overview of the theological issues at stake, but it does not devote much space to the issues of practice.

5. Finney, *Lectures,* p. 326. The lecture on testifying by one's life is the ninth in the series, pp. 140–55. Finney warns against "waiting for certain feelings, which somebody else has had. . . . This is very common in revivals, where some one of the first converts has told of remarkable experiences" (p. 167).

6. William Sprague, *Lectures on Revivals of Religion* (2nd ed.; New York: Daniel Appleton & Co., 1833). The identification with orthodoxy appears in the preface. The second edition of this work is valuable because Sprague included in it some letters solicited from other New England ministers to support his positions as to what constituted

a proper revival. Some of those are useful for their insights into, and comments upon, prevailing practices, and are cited in notes below.

7. Ibid., pp. 4–5, 83–86.

8. Testimony was prominent in the meetings of the Lane Seminary abolitionists (1830s), for example, especially when given by former slaveholders; and it was the primary attraction among the "Washingtonians" in the temperance movement (1840s). On the former, see Donald M. Scott, *From Office to Profession: The New England Ministry, 1750–1850* (Philadelphia: University of Pennsylvania Press, 1978); on the latter, Donald A. Koch, Introduction to Timothy Shay Arthur's *Ten Nights in a Bar-room, and What I Saw There* (1854; rpt. John Harvard Library Series; Cambridge: Harvard University Press, 1964), pp. lvi–lvii. Both groups were strongly influenced by revivals, the former by converts of Finney, the latter by Jacob Knapp.

9. "Convention," pp. 361–64.

10. Finney, *Lectures,* chs. 6–8, pp. 45–128.

11. For an example, see ibid., p. 110. On Finney's view of man's will and God's, see Sweet, "View of Man," pp. 207–10.

12. Finney, *Lectures,* pp. 81, 60, 94, 114.

13. Charles G. Finney, "Christian Affinity," in *Sermons on Important Subjects* (New York: John S. Taylor, 1836), pp. 186–204.

14. Ibid., p. 186.

15. Ibid., p. 190; cf. Finney, *Lectures,* p. 115. This quotation supports Sweet's view that Finney's "new measures" were largely a matter of a new style. Sweet also argues that Finney was concerned not only with feelings but with the intellectual operations of the mind ("Views of Man," pp. 214–15). That is evidenced by many of Finney's sermons. But as "Christian Affinity" shows, Finney was at this point more concerned with changing the feelings in order to change the will and with the practice and moral behavior that emanated from like feeling.

16. Finney, "Christian Affinity," p. 197.

17. See, for example, Lyman Beecher, letter to the *Christian Observer* (London) 28 (1828): 538.

18. Sprague, *Lectures,* p. 85.

19. Beecher, letter to *Christian Observer,* p. 474.

20. For a discussion of the importance of order and decorum in understanding cultural systems, see the work of anthropologist Mary Douglas, especially *Purity and Danger: An Analysis of Concepts of Pollution and Taboo* (rev. ed.; Baltimore: Penguin Books, 1970).

21. The entire letter was printed in two parts, Aug. and Sept. 1828, pp. 473–81, 537–44.

22. Ibid., pp. 480–81.

23. Ibid., p. 538. Compare the complaint of Albert Dod, a theologian who attacked Finney's *Lectures* in a review published in Princeton's *Biblical Repertory and Theological Review* 7 (1835): 633–34 (and quoted in McLoughlin's introduction to Finney, *Lectures,* pp. xxxix–xl): " . . . Everywhere the social mass is seen to be in such a state of agitation that the slightest breath may make it heave and foam. . . . Should religion fall in with the excitement and institute measures for fostering it . . . ? We had thought that one great object of religion was to allay this undue excitement of the human mind; to check its feverish outgoings toward earthy objects and to teach it without hurry or distraction, in self-collectedness, to put forth its energies in a proper direction and to their best advantage."

Such sentiments were common among the older evangelicals. It is interesting to contrast their models of order, based on a notion of "civilization" which has European overtones (decorum and courtesy, and the primary contrast being between "Christian" and "savage" nations) with that of later ones. Even Beecher's own *Plea for the West* (1835) has a different tone; and by the time we reach his daughter's *Uncle Tom's Cabin* (1852), the ideal model of order is distinctively Western, or more precisely Ohioan, with overtones from the frontier's rough edges and the unpolished stones of Africa. The frontier image has received considerable attention of course, but it would be interesting to investigate in a more extensive way the "cosmography" of Americans at different periods: attitudes toward Europe, Asia, Africa, as well as toward the frontier and toward the American Indians who lived there. For a recent and provocative interpretation of the frontier ideology, see Catherine Albanese, "Citizen Crockett: Myth, History and Nature Religion," *Soundings* 61 (1978): 87–104.

24. Beecher, letter to *Christian Observer,* pp. 540–41, 542, 543.

25. Cotton Mather, *Ratio Disciplinae Fratrum Nov-Anglorum* (Boston: n.p., 1726), p. 53. John Cotton, too, admitted that a "private Christian" who had a musical gift could write and sing a hymn "for his own private comfort, and remembrance of some speciall benefit or deliverance"; and even, if he composed a psalm (that is, a psalm tune), could "sing it before the Church, and the rest hearing it, and approving it, may goe along with him in the Spirit, and say Amen to it." But Cotton never mentioned the use of *hymns* in public worship. See *Singing of Psalms a Gospel Ordinance* (Boston: n.p., 1726), quoted in George Hood, *A History of Music in New England* (Boston: Wilkins, Carter & Co., 1846), p. 38.

26. Mather, *Ratio,* p. 53.

27. Harry Escott, *Isaac Watts, Hymnographer* (London: Independent Press, 1962), pp. 150–53.

28. Henry Wilder Foote, *Three Centuries of American Hymnody* (Cambridge: Harvard University Press, 1940), pp. 65–68.

29. Scott, *Office to Profession,* gives the best description; see also Perry Miller, *The Life of the Mind in America: From the Revolution to the Civil War* (New York: Harcourt, Brace & World, 1965), pp. 3–35.

30. The influence of an urban Methodism has been suggested by Richard Carwadine, "The Second Great Awakening in the Urban Centers: An Examination of Methodism and the 'New Measures,'" *Journal of American History* 59 (1972–73): 327–40. For sources on the frontier hymns, see Chapter 1, note 15; for other English sources in circulation, consult Louis Benson, *The English Hymn: Its Development and Use in Worship* (New York: Hodder & Stoughton, 1915), pp. 315–40. Standard church hymnody in New England was still largely limited to "revisions" of Watts and often was still referred to as psalmody; on these see Foote, *Three Centuries,* pp. 187–89.

31. Asahel Nettleton, Preface to *Village Hymns for Social Worship* (1824; rpt. stereotype ed.; Hartford, Conn.: Brown and Parsons, 1850, pp. vi, viii. For discussions of *Village Hymns* and the other revival hymnals described below, see Benson, *English Hymn,* pp. 358–79, and Foote, *Three Centuries,* pp. 190–208.

32. Joshua Leavitt, Preface to *The Christian Lyre* (1831; rpt., New York: Dayton and Saxton, 1842), p. 3.

33. Thomas Hastings and Lowell Mason, Preface to *Spiritual Songs for Social Worship* (Utica, N.Y.: Hastings & Tracy & W. Williams, 1832), pp. 4–6. Gilbert Chase points out that the models for their music were primarily European (*America's Music: From the Pilgrims to the Present* [New York: McGraw-Hill Book Co., 1955], pp. 154–57).

34. Hastings and Mason, Preface to *Spiritual Songs,* p. 3.

35. For a description of the kinds of meetings frequently used, see the letter from Francis Wayland to William Sprague, March 7, 1832, in Sprague, *Lectures,* pp. 237–38. He mentions, for example, families who live in the same neighborhood; particular "classes" such as parents, fathers, mothers, young men, young men in business, middle-aged persons, meetings for conference or exhortation for lay brethren, Bible classes.

36. Sprague, *Lectures,* pp. 191–93. Cf. the letters from Charles P. McIlvaine, p. 311, and Daniel Dana, p. 246. Finney gave a brief warning about ignoring closet duties in his *Lectures,* p. 265.

37. On the system of benevolent societies, see John R. Bodo, *The Protestant Clergy and Public Issues, 1812–1848* (Princeton, N.J.: Princeton University Press, 1954); Charles C. Cole, Jr., *The Social Ideas of the Northern Evangelists, 1826–1860* (Columbia Studies in the Social Sciences, No. 580; New York: Columbia University Press, 1954); Charles I. Foster, *An Errand of Mercy: The Evangelical United Front, 1790–1837* (Chapel Hill, N.C.: University of North Carolina Press, 1960); and Clifford S. Griffin, *Their Brothers' Keepers: Moral Stewardship in the United States, 1800–1865* (New Brunswick, N.J.: Rutgers University Press, 1960); for a critique, see Lois W. Banner, "Religious Benevolence as Social Control: A Critique of an Interpretation," *Journal of American History* 60 (1973): 23–41.

38. The quotations are from Leonard L. Richards, *"Gentlemen of Property and Standing": Anti-Abolition Mobs in Jacksonian America* (New York: Oxford University Press, 1970), p. 59; see especially his ch. 3, and also Lorman Ratner, *Powder Keg: Northern Opposition to the Antislavery Movement 1831–1840* (New York: Basic Books, 1968). The classic on the Anti-Slavery Society is Gilbert Barnes, *The Anti-Slavery Impulse, 1830–1844* (1933; rpt., New York: Harcourt, Brace & World, 1961), still well worth reading. William G. McLoughlin's introduction to the 1964 paperback edition provides a good summary of the weaknesses later scholars have found in Barnes's treatment. On "immediatism," see David Brion Davis, "The Emergence of Immediatism in British and American Anti-Slavery Thought," *Mississippi Valley Historical Review* 49 (1962–63): 209–30.

39. For discussion of these difficulties, see Bertram Wyatt–Brown, "Prelude to Abolitionism: Sabbatarian Politics and the Rise of the Second Party System," *Journal of American History* 58 (1971–72): 316–41.

40. Calvin Colton, *Protestant Jesuitism* (New York: Harper & Brothers, 1836). It was originally written anonymously, "by a Protestant." For a survey of Colton's ideas, see Alfred A. Cave, *An American Conservative in the Age of Jackson: The Political and Social Thought of Calvin Colton* (Fort Worth, Tex.: Texas Christian University Press, 1969).

41. Colton, *Jesuitism,* p. 15. The comparison with Catholicism is made in a different way by Edward D. Griffin in his letter in Sprague, *Lectures,* p. 369: "Truth has to do with reason and conscience, but these tactics with imagination and passion first, and afterwards with a stupid reliance on forms, as the whole history of the church attests. . . . The frequent repetition of these imposing ceremonies [e.g., when a whole assembly is called to kneel] will destroy their effect, and leave us with forms instead of feelings. It was in this way that the primitive

church sunk into all the dead formalities of the church of Rome. The ceremonies were first adopted because they were thought to be impressive. In time they ceased to impress, and then the magnificent and garnished body of worship was accepted for the soul."

42. Colton, *Jesuitism,* pp. 96–97.

43. Ibid., p. 52.

44. Richards has hypothesized that improvements in printing which made it much cheaper to spread tracts was an important factor in the attitudes toward abolitionism's "machinery"; see *"Gentlemen,"* Ch. 3.

45. Calvin Colton, *Thoughts on the Religious State of the Country; with Reasons for Preferring Episcopacy* (2nd ed.; New York: Harper & Brothers, 1836), pp. 177–78. Cf. McIlvaine's letter in Sprague, *Lectures,* pp. 308–9: "A revival has been represented and sought for as an article of manufacture, for which you have only to set the machinery and raise the steam of excitement, caring little with what fuel, and converts will be made to hand." Even Finney, writing "Letters on Revivals" in the *Oberlin Evangelist* in 1845 and 1846, had decided that revivals had become too "mechanical" in nature (see McLoughlin, Introduction to Finney, *Lectures,* pp. xlix—lii). *Contra* Richards, mentioned in the preceding note, it seems likely that all this talk of machinery had more to do with the rise of industrialism in general than with any specific example of it, as in printing—although that certainly could have heightened its impact on particular groups.

46. Calvin Colton, *A Voice from America to England, by an American Gentleman* (London: Henry Colburn, 1839), pp. 94–95.

47. Ibid., p. 87.

48. Quoted from the American Sunday-School Union, *Anniversary Sermons* (Philadelphia: American Sunday-School Union, 1860), pp. 26–27. Similar language can be found in Lyman Beecher, "The Perils of Atheism to the Nation," *Works* (3 vols.; Boston: John P. Jewett & Company, 1852–53), vol. 1. On the attacks of evangelicals on politics, see Wyatt-Brown, "Prelude"; he also argues that they adopted many of the politicans' tactics themselves. Ronald P. Formisano, in his *The Birth of Mass Political Parties: Michigan, 1827–1861* (Princeton, N.J.: Princeton University Press, 1971) suggests that political parties learned their techniques from the evangelicals, Whig campaigns being a kind of political revivalism (p. 133). Formisano also provides excellent examples of anti-party, anti-organization rhetoric among evangelicals and Whigs (see esp. Ch. 4).

49. See David Brion Davis, "Some Themes of Counter-Subversion: An Analysis of Anti-Masonic, Anti-Catholic, and Anti-Mormon Litera-

ture," *Mississippi Valley Historical Review* 49 (1960–61): 205–24. For a history of anti-Catholicism and related movements, see the standard work by Ray Allen Billington, *The Protestant Crusade, 1800–1860* (Chicago: Quadrangle Books, 1938).

50. Griffin, *Brothers' Keepers,* p. 64. On the "interlocking directorates" of the societies, see Barnes, *Anti-Slavery,* ch. 2; Cole, *Social Ideas,* p. 103; and Foster, *Errand,* pp. 154–55 (*contra* Clifford S. Griffin in *the Ferment of Reform, 1830–1860* [New York: Crowell, 1967], who says Foster disagrees with the Barnes consensus on that issue).

51. John Higham, *From Boundlessness to Consolidation: The Transformation of American Culture, 1848–1860* (Ann Arbor, Mich.: William L. Clements Library, 1969). Higham is one of the few historians to argue that the major cultural changes of the nineteenth century came before the Civil War, not after (although many historians who emphasize economic determinants have focused on the prewar period because of the intensive industrialization). On the basis of my studies in evangelicalism, I would heartily agree. The emergence of the evangelical novel, of the Sunday-school hymns on which the gospel hymns were based, and of the mass urban revival form (with the exception of the Moody-style sermon) all occurred during the decade 1850–60. Cf. Scott, *Office to Profession,* and on politics and religion see Formisano, *Mass Political Parties.*

52. See especially Formisano, *Mass Political Parties,* for evidence from Michigan.

53. On hymnals, see Benson, *English Hymn,* pp. 390–429, and Foote, *Three Centuries,* pp. 213–62. Colton was, naturally, one of those who advocated a return to an ecclesiastical focus; see *Jesuitism,* pp. 113–38. William Bean Kennedy, in his *The Shaping of Protestant Education* (New York: Association Press, 1966), points out that most churches had reverted to a denominational emphasis in the Sunday schools before 1860 (pp. 72–74). Of course, the 1837 schism in the Presbyterian Church is the standard illustration of the division between the two camps. In another area one can see the influence of a conservative concern for maintaining social order—namely, in the reformers who dealt with criminals, the poor, and the insane. See the interesting study by David Rothman, *The Discovery of the Asylum: Social Order and Disorder in the New Republic* (Boston: Little, Brown and Co., 1971). The "reformers" Rothman discusses seem to have been most interested in preserving the old order although through new, separate institutions of prison, almshouse, and asylum. They emphasized discipline and control—and for this reason, interestingly, criticized the "soft" atti-

tude toward child-raising espoused by many of their contemporaries. In sharp contrast to the evangelicals who, as we will see in the next two chapters, eulogized the family, they criticized it harshly.

54. Leonard Woods, "Present Ecclesiastical and Religious Condition of Christendom," *American Biblical Repository* 10 (1837): 29.

55. Ibid., pp. 30–31.

56. Cf. Higham's comments on architects of a new consolidation, *Boundlessness,* p. 26.

Chapter 4
Passion in its Place: The Domestic Image

1. Social historians are beginning to study these changes in detail, with particular relevance to economic structures and changes in work patterns with the advent of industrialism. See, for example, Edward Pessen, *Riches, Class, and Power Before the Civil War* (Lexington, Mass.: D.C. Heath and Company, 1973). The best study of relationships between social changes and evangelical and reform movements, however, remains Whitney Cross's *The Burned Over District: The Social and Intellectual History of Enthusiastic Religion in Western New York, 1800–1850* (Ithaca, N.Y.: Cornell University Press, 1950; rpt. New York: Harper & Row, 1961), now nearly thirty years old.

2. Ronald P. Formisano, in *The Birth of Mass Political Parties: Michigan, 1827–1861* (Princeton, N.J.: Princeton University Press, 1971), has shown clearly the parallelism of evangelicalism and politics. Faced with the fact of political parties, evangelicals (even party Whigs) appealed to the importance of conscience and individual judgment. Conversely, as we saw in the last chapter, politicians faced with powerful benevolent societies accused them of dictatorship. Moreover, Formisano argues, the dualism of evangelicalism (like Finney's in the last chapter), channeled through Antimasonry, fueled the idea of party regularity (p. 67).

3. William G. McLoughlin, Jr., *Modern Revivalism: Charles Grandison Finney to Billy Graham* (New York: Ronald Press, 1959), pp. 160–61. His book provides a good discussion of the leading revivalists between Finney and Moody; see also Timothy L. Smith, *Revivalism and Social Reform* (New York: Harper and Row, 1965), ch. 3. The Civil War period, however, remains largely untouched, even though the Southern armies experienced considerable revival activity and the Northern armies were ministered to (but not, apparently, revived) by the Christian Commission. On the former, see Herman Norton, "Revivalism in

the Confederate Armies," *Civil War History* 6 (1960): 410–24; on the latter, James O. Henry, "The United States Christian Commission in the Civil War," ibid., pp. 374–88.

4. Ann Douglas, *The Feminization of American Culture* (New York: Alfred A. Knopf, 1977). Cf. Nancy Cott, "Women and the Clergy, 1790–1830," lecture delivered at Princeton Seminary, March 29, 1978 (available on tape).

5. Revivalism from Finney's time onward appealed to many classes. Methodists and Baptists at first attracted the less settled, less well-educated frontiersmen and immigrants; but by mid-century the gap between these denominations and the established ones had narrowed. Both had established colleges and seminaries, and most of their leaders had moved away from the exuberance of famous preachers like Methodist Peter Cartwright. In a society which was, despite the egalitarian ideology, somewhat stratified, the evangelicals may have been located toward the low end of the middle-cass spectrum. But they were far from illiterate: their periodicals were alive and well; their members contributed significantly to the emerging body of popular literature, as is evidenced in the authorship of the lyrics of *Gospel Hymns.* Until more careful social and demographic analysis appears, we cannot make hasty judgments as to the composition of evangelical churches in mid-century. The literature suggests that, whatever the actual socioeconomic status of church members and clergy, their ideals were thoroughly middle class, in harmony with that described by Douglas for the liberals from a more elitist tradition. For indications about class, religion, and politics in Michigan, see Formisano, *Mass Political Parties,* Chs. 3 and 8.

6. This, as Douglas observes (*Feminization,* pp. 98–99), was nothing new, insofar as women had often dominated New England churches numerically. In this period, as they became consumers of popular literature, they became an effective source of constraint on the ministers.

7. For a description of the various features of women's participation, see also Barbara Welter, "The Feminization of American Religion, 1800–1860," in *Insights and Parallels: Problems and Issues of American Social History,* ed. William L. O'Neill (Minneapolis: Burgess Publishing Co., 1973).

8. I adopt the term "insulation" in the sense used by Mary Douglas, in her essay "Cosmology," to describe people whose roles are carefully prescribed and who are cut off from interaction with others. For readers interested in her theory, I might add the following comments:

Obviously the nineteenth-century women and clergy were not totally insulated; they do not represent an extreme case (such as that of a live-in maid with no external associations and no significant interaction with the family who employs her services). They were nevertheless located toward the high-grid/weak-group quadrant insofar as they were insulated from political and economic decision-making processes in the larger society. The more this was the case, the less one would expect them to have developed a distinctive cosmology.

But there is another way of portraying the situation. Insofar as women and clergy then created out of their own resources—in churches, in reform societies, in mass literature—a separate sphere for themselves, they would look more like a low-grid/strong-group type. Their relative autonomy within their own realm would reduce grid. If they accepted the role definitions imposed by the larger society (as mother, as minister) and used those to create a positive identification with their group, they would be increasingly justifying their behavior in terms of their membership in this group. The more they were involved in this sphere, church and home, the stronger the group would be; for, as Douglas puts it, group strength in measured in terms of "how much of the individual's life is absorbed in and sustained by group membership" ("Cosmology," p. 19). (We see here that insulation, a variable along the line of grid, can become part of a definition of strength of group. This suggests again that the variables are not fully independent, as I suggested in Chapter 1, note 27.) Unlike the small-sect example, however, the boundary against "outsiders," that is, nonclerical men, was not well maintained. The reasons are obvious: most women and clergy were at least partly dependent on men for financial resources; the women lived with men in the home, where their defined roles (which now they attempted to transform into positive identities) were always ones which related them to men ("wife," "mother," etc.). The clergy and women show evidence of wanting to contribute to the larger society (through moral reform) and/or to draw men into their realm (through conversion). The boundaries were clear but they were not impermeable.

We have here a mixed case: partial insulation, clear but weak group boundaries. The cosmology that the group produced, as evidenced in the novels described in this chapter, is interesting as well. It looks most like Douglas's description of low-grid/strong-group cosmology. Sharply dualistic, it portrays the larger society of business and politics as evil, while the home and family (regarded as 'natural," God-ordained) are good. Parts of "nature" are evil and threatening also, insofar as nature exemplifies wild passions and impulses in free play. But victims can be saved by being brought within the realm of home and family. The women and clergy even produced their own demonology in the form of "demon rum" which excites the evil passions. The home became an arena where women and clergy presided over and even gloried in sickness and death. One could cite other characteristics that fit with the type. But it should also be noted that the group retained an individualistic ideology from the larger competitive society (low-grid/weak-group), and some of its values as, for example, positive values for health, youth, and beauty. One might suggest that these latter come to the fore when members of the group had to compete with or defend themselves against the larger society; careful examination of evidence is necessary to test that suggestion.

Most importantly, this particular group developed an ideology in which they saw themselves not only as the "elect," so to speak, as in most small sects, but also as saviors for the larger society, as a channel of redemptive power. Mary Douglas does not consider this possibility, but it is interesting for her theory. One might put it as follows: when members of a (partly) insulated group create a positive identification with their own insulation, they tend to move toward the weak-grid/strong-group quadrant; but because of their partial interaction with and dependence on the larger society, boundaries are weak. This produces a cosmology in which they see themselves as vehicles of redemption or spirituality for the whole society. It would be interesting to look for comparable cases. One might consider, for example, some figures who came out of the black subculture during the periods of slavery or segregation. I think of W. E. B. DuBois, who clearly articulated at some points in his life a messianic vision of blacks as the hope of the world. One might inquire also into the social conditions under which Israelite spokesmen generated an image of Israel as "light to the nations." And so on. Thus, the present case reveals some interesting complications that can emerge within the framework of Mary Douglas's theory.

9. For an excellent description of changes in women's work patterns, see Nancy Cott, *The Bonds of Womanhood: "Woman's Sphere" in New England, 1780–1835* (New Haven: Yale University Press, 1977). Ch. 1.

10. Again, males who were not clergy did participate in creating and maintaining this sphere—not only literary men like T. S. Arthur, whom we will consider below, but leaders of the Sunday-school movement, the musicians mentioned in Chapter 1 who wrote the tunes for

Gospel Hymns, and others. Precisely what their backgrounds were and what effects they had must remain for future study. Perusal of the literature suggests, however, that most of those who wrote for the mass market wrote within the sphere of evangelical domesticity. (I am obviously excluding major figures like Whitman and Melville.) They wrote for women. As Ann Douglas observes, quoting writer Nathaniel Willis, "It is the women who read. It is the women who are the tribunal of any question aside from politics or business. It is the women who give or withhold a literary reputation. It is the women who regulate the style of living. . . . It is the women who exercise the ultimate control over the Press" (*Feminization,* p. 103).

11. Ik Marvel (Donald Grant Mitchell), *Reveries of a Bachelor; or, a Book of the Heart* (3rd ed.; New York: Baker and Scribner, 1851), p. 90.

12. Walter Houghton, *The Victorian Frame of Mind, 1830–1870* (New Haven: Yale University Press, 1957), p. 343. There has been a great deal of work in recent years on the domestic ideology, besides the efforts by Ann Douglas, Barbara Welter, and Nancy Cott cited previously. With special reference to the evangelical world, see Kathryn Sklar, *Catharine Beecher: A Study in Domesticity* (New Haven: Yale University Press, 1973). Cushing Strout, in his *The New Heavens and New Earth: Political Religion in America* (New York: Harper & Row, 1974), mentions the "cult of the family" as "illustrative of the underlining ethical impulse of the whole humanitarian reform movement of the ante-bellum period" (p. 182), but he does not develop it in the direction of the ideology of the passions.

On the domestic and female images in general see Kirk Jeffrey, "The Family as Utopian Retreat from the City: The Nineteenth Century Contribution," in *The Family, Communes, and Utopian Societies,* ed. Sallie TeSelle (New York: Harper & Row, 1971), pp. 21–41; Anne Firor Scott, *The Southern Lady* (Chicago: University of Chicago Press, 1970); William R. Taylor, *Cavalier and Yankee* (New York: Harper & Row, 1961), ch. 4; Charles E. Rosenberg, "Sexuality, Class and Role in Nineteenth-Century America," *American Quarterly* 25 (1973): 131–54; Carroll Smith Rosenberg, "Beauty, the Beast and the Militant Woman: A Case Study in Sex Roles and Social Stress in Jacksonian America," *American Quarterly* 23 (1971): 562–84, which does emphasize the relation to evangelicalism of a stronger feminine image; and Barbara Welter, "The Cult of True Womanhood, 1800–1860," *American Quarterly* 18 (1966): 151–74. For perspectives on other aspects of the woman's world, see William R. Taylor and Christopher Lasch, "Two 'Kindred Spirits'; Sorority and Family in New England, 1839–1846,"

New England Quarterly 36 (1963): 23–41; and Carroll Smith Rosenberg, "The Female World of Love and Ritual: Relations between Women in Nineteenth-Century America," *Signs* 1 (1975): 1–29; also the essays in Mary Hartman and Lois W. Banner, eds., *Clio's Consciousness Raised: New Perspectives on the History of Women* (New York: Harper & Row, 1974). Literary studies include Herbert Ross Brown, *The Sentimental Novel in America, 1789–1860* (Durham, N.C.: Duke University Press, 1940); Alexander Cowie, *The Rise of the American Novel* (New York: American Book Co., 1948); Helen Papashvily, *All the Happy Endings* (New York: Harper & Row, 1956); and Edward Branch, *The Sentimental Years, 1836–1860* (New York: Hill and Wang, 1932). See also James D. Hart, *The Popular Book: A History of America's Literary Taste* (Berkeley and Los Angeles: University of California Press, 1963), ch. 6 and his bibliography.

13. Nineteenth-century ambivalence toward emotion and its control shows itself subtly in images of the female psyche, as demonstrated in the following studies: Carroll Smith Rosenberg, "The Hysterical Woman: Sex Roles and Role Conflict in Nineteenth Century America," *Social Research* 39 (1972): 652–78, and her "Puberty to Menopause: The Cycle of Femininity in Nineteenth-Century America," *Feminist Studies* 1 (1973): 53–69; Carroll Smith Rosenberg and Charles Rosenberg, "The Female Animal: Medical and Biological Views of Women in Nineteenth Century America," *Journal of American History* 60 (1973): 332–56; Carl N. Degler, "Women's Sexuality in the Nineteenth Century," *American Historical Review* 79 (1974): 1469–90.

14. Timothy Shay Arthur, *Ten Nights in a Bar-room, and What I Saw There* (1854; rpt. John Harvard Library; Cambridge: Harvard University Press, 1964); this edition contains an excellent introduction by Donald A. Koch. Page references in the discussion which follows are given only to the longer quotations, in parentheses immediately following. For discussion of the temperance novel, see Brown, *Sentimental Novel,* pp. 201–40.

15. It is interesting to observe, in the novels' descriptions of characters, the economic correlates of the other aspects of their personalities. A villain cannot be an ordinary businessman who happens to have a sinister streak; he must be rootless, of unknown occupation, a gambler. Heroes will almost always be self-made men, while heroines tend to be heiresses of wealth. Extremes of wealth are generally bad, although it is better to be poor than to be rich, at least until late in the century. All this is significant, in part because it reveals the distinctively middle-class bias of evangelicalism. It also raises the question of

the relation of this aspect of popular ideology to the others which I am discussing. Clearly, attitudes toward money and wealth are connected, often explicitly, with the state of the passions or affections; characters have a *lust* for profit, for example. The connection between passion and property runs very deep in evangelical ideology, and it deserves to be investigated more fully.

16. Mary is described as "full of a tender concern that had its origin too deep for the heart of a child" and as "more like a guardian angel than a child" (pp. 23, 73). She is one of the classic and rather maudlin figures of nineteenth-century fiction: the innocent child who dies a happy death, thereby effecting the conversion of others; the mother may play the same role. Compare, for example, the figure of Evangeline in *Uncle Tom's Cabin.*

17. John William Ward, Afterword to Harriet Beecher Stowe, *Uncle Tom's Cabin* (1852; rpt., New York: New American Library, Signet Books, 1966), p. 485.

18. Stowe, *Cabin,* p. 472.

19. Ward, Afterword to ibid., p. 490.

20. Edward Payson Roe, *Barriers Burned Away* (New York: Dodd & Mead, 1872). Page references to the longer quotations appear in parentheses immediately following. Roe was a New York Presbyterian pastor turned novelist; for some biographical information, see E. P. Roe, "A Native Author Called Roe," *Lippincott's Magazine* 41 (1888): 479–94.

21. In a later bestseller, *Opening a Chestnut Burr* (New York: Dodd & Mead, 1874), Roe uses music and especially hymns as the vehicle of feeling, along with home and woman, and his climactic device at the end is a shipwreck.

Roe's use of all this imagery contextualizes somewhat a famous example of language from the same period: the poem, Emma Lazarus's "The New Colossus" (1883), inscribed on the Statue of Liberty, which also emphasizes the redemptive role of woman, favorable attitudes toward the poor, and negative ones toward Old Europe:

> Not like the brazen giant of Greek fame,
> With conquering limbs astride from land to land;
> Here at our sea-washed, sunset gates shall stand
> A mighty woman with a torch, whose flame
> Is the imprisoned lightning, and her name
> Mother of Exiles. From her beacon-hand
> Glows world-wide welcome; her mild eyes command
> The air-bridged harbor that twin cities frame.

"Keep, ancient lands, your storied pomp!" cries she
With silent lips. "Give me your tired, your poor,
Your huddled masses yearning to breathe free,
The wretched refuse of your teeming shore.
Send these, the homeless, tempest-tost to me,
I lift my lamp beside the golden door!"

Lazarus's imagery expresses in a remarkably condensed and powerful way the ideology of domesticity: the woman, Mother of Exiles, is unlike the conquering giant of the old Colossus; she rules, but with "mild eyes" and "silent lips." The torch is the "imprisoned lightning"—a perfect symbol for intense feeling, perfectly controlled. And, like Bliss's "lights along the shore," she lifts that lamp so that the "homeless, tempest-tost" can find their way home.

For the history of the inscription, see John Higham, *Send These to Me: Jews and Other Immigrants in Urban America* (New York: Atheneum, 1975), ch. 4.

22. Wayne Elzey, " 'What Would Jesus Do?' *In His Steps* and the Moral Codes of the Middle Class," *Soundings* 58 (1975): 463–89.

23. Charles Sheldon, *In His Steps* (New York: J. H. Sears & Co., 1896). An alternative approach to the same problem appears in *The Silent Partner* by Elizabeth Stuart Phelps [Ward] (Boston: J. R. Osgood and Co., 1871), probably one of the first American novels to take up directly the theme of social reform. Her heroine, an upper-class heiress, grows concerned about the plight of the poor and visits the slums, but her chief tactic is to have them to her home for social gatherings, to expose them to "culture." But there is also a lower-class counterpart heroine who aims to save her comrades by preaching to them. Unlike Phelp's "heaven" novels, this never became a bestseller. Perhaps her notions of reform were too direct and unromantic; but also, the book had a thoroughgoing feminist attitude which undoubtedly would have offended many in the 1870s.

24. Claude Lévi-Strauss, *Totemism,* trans. Rodney Needham (Boston: Beacon Press, 1963; orig. pub. as *Le Totémisme aujourd'hui*; 1962), p. 89: "natural species are chosen not because they are 'good to eat' but because they are 'good to think.' " In the French, there is a double pun: not only "good" but "goods" to eat or think with; or, a voucher for goods—emphasizing the function of items in exchange.

Chapter 5
The Taming of the Spirit: The New Urban Revivals

1. In this period, unlike the later social-gospel era, the term "social

Christianity" was used in much the same way as I used "social religion"—devotional meetings designed to increase Christians' growth in grace and concern for each other's spiritual welfare and also for Bible study groups. See Old South Church, Boston, *Old South Chapel Prayer Meeting: Its Origin and History* (2nd ed.; Boston: J. E. Tilton & Co., 1859), pp. 46–57. On the Sunday school, see Robert W. Lynn and Elliott Wright, *The Big Little School: Sunday Child of American Protestantism* (New York: Harper & Row, 1971), esp. pp. 56–76. As McLoughlin has pointed out, the Sunday-school movement of the 1850–75 period was still devotion and conversion oriented, having not yet adopted Horace Bushnell's theory of Christian nurture even though his writings on the subject were available (*Modern Revivalism: Charles Grandison Finney to Billy Graham* [New York: Ronald Press, 1959], p. 157). For the emphasis on the Sunday schools' close relationship to the home circle (while not attempting to replace it, as was always carefully stressed) see the later sermons in American Sunday-School Union, *Anniversary Sermons* (Philadelphia: American Sunday-School Union, 1860).

2. Quoted from the original Boston constitution and by-laws by C. Howard Hopkins, *History of the Y.M.C.A. in North America* (New York: Association Press, 1951), p. 18.

3. Moody toured the country from 1875 to 1881, when he left to visit Britain again, but in 1878 he shifted to smaller towns and the campaign was less well publicized; after that, he changed his approach, staying in a city for a longer time but preaching in churches. His reputation remained strong, but the furor of the enormous revivals had died down by the end of 1877. For the changes in method, see James F. Findlay, Jr., *Dwight L. Moody: American Evangelist, 1837–1899* (Chicago: University of Chicago Press, 1969), pp. 303–6.

4. S. Irenaeus Prime, *Fifteen Years of Prayer in the Fulton Street Meeting* (New York: Scribner, Armstrong, & Co., 1872), p. 20.

5. John Hall and George H. Stuart, *The American Evangelists, D. L. Moody and Ira D. Sankey, in Great Britain and Ireland* (New York: Dodd & Mead, 1875), p. 115; cf. Prime, *Fifteen Years,* pp. 256, 326.

6. Henry C. Fish, *Handbook of Revivals: For the Use of Winners of Souls* (Boston: James H. Earle, 1874), pp. 134, 319; William C. Conant, *Narratives of Remarkable Conversions and Revival Incidents* (New York: Derby & Jackson, 1858), p. 416; *Old South Meeting,* p. 12; E. J. Goodspeed, *The Wonderful Career of Moody and Sankey in Great Britain and America* (New York: Henry Goodspeed, 1876), p. 383; cf. Prime, *Fifteen Years,* p. 267, on the spirit spreading like fire, from one heart to another.

7. Charles Lemuel Thompson, *Times of Refreshing: A History of American Revivals* (Chicago: L. T. Palmer & Co., 1877), p. 319; cf. *Old South Meeting,* p. 47.

8. Prime, *Fifteen Years,* p. 27; Fish, *Handbook,* p. 400; Conant, *Narratives,* pp. 416, 394–95; cf. *Old South Meeting,* p. 152: "The heart is the telegraph wire over which prayer ascends to heaven, and gracious answer speedily returns."

9. An exception is Conant's return to the flood metaphor, in an imperialistic-sounding expression of hope: "Conceive the effect of this swelling wave of Divine influence as it sweeps around the globe, upon the many families of the earth, docile Nestorians, inquiring Bulgarians, susceptible Karens, Fejee Islanders, etc., who are waiting for the kingdom of God, or already pressing into it" (*Narratives,* p. 415).

10. That the meetings were intended for businessmen—that is, for the middle class—is shown by the fact that they were an hour long; at that time factory workers had only half an hour for lunch. Some accounts mention that some workingmen came to the meetings on their lunch break, but that suggests it was rare enough to deserve mention.

It was not only prayer meetings but prayer as a whole that became an important focus during this period. One finds a profusion of books beginning in the late 1850s on subjects like "the power of prayer" and "the still hour." It was also at this time that an interdenominational "Week of Prayer" was instituted; see Prime, *Fifteen Years,* p. 21, and Fish, *Handbook,* p. 298.

11. Conant, *Narratives,* pp. 380–82; cf. Frank Beardsley's similar description of a Philadelphia prayer meeting in *A History of American Revivals* (3rd ed., rev. and enl.; New York: American Tract Society, 1912), p. 233. Conant (p. 396) notes that the revival created a great demand for inexpensive hymnals; the one in use in New York was a Sunday-school songbook.

12. Conant, *Narratives,* Prime, *Fifteen Years,* and *Old South Meeting* all give many examples.

13. The pattern of the revivals was basically the same in Britain and America. Many accounts in newspapers and books describe the various sorts of meetings; I have collated material mainly from Hall and Stuart, *Evangelists,* and Goodspeed, *Wonderful Career*; see also the descriptions by McLoughlin in *Modern Revivalism,* pp. 231–62. For a description of a typical one-day meeting in a small town, see Hall and Stuart, *Evangelists,* p. 188.

14. Conant, *Narratives,* p. 357n.; cf. Harvey Newcomb, *The Harvest*

and the Reapers: Home-work for All, and How to Do It (Boston: Gould and Lincoln, 1858), pp. 210–16.

15. Fish, *Handbook,* p. 299.

16. Ibid., pp. 242–43: cf. p. 252.

17. Quoted in Goodspeed, *Wonderful Career,* p. 397; cf. Moody's comment in the sermon, "Confessing Christ," in *Glad Tidings: Comprising Sermons and Prayer-Meeting Talks, Delivered at the N.Y. Hippodrome* (New York: E. B. Treat, 1876), p. 187: "If a man is converted I want him to come here and give his experience. . ., and the result may be that God will use his witnessing to the conversion of many."

18. Thompson, *Times,* pp. 382–83. Some worried, as had Finney, about the tendency this created toward mere imitation. Henry Ward Beecher, writing the introduction to Conant's *Narratives,* warned that young people and new Christians "should be taught not to try themselves by other people's evidences. . . . Do not lose comfort and growth in grace by waiting to feel like some other Christian" (pp. xvi–xvii).

19. Goodspeed, *Wonderful Career,* p. 234.

20. Conant, *Narratives,* p. 391.

21. Dwight L. Moody, "The Pharisee and the Publican," in *Great Joy: Comprising Sermons and Prayer-Meeting Talks, Delivered at the Chicago Tabernacle* (New York: E. B. Treat, 1877), pp. 390–91. We do not know the sources of Moody's stories, but it is interesting to find that one of his favorites, that of a Catholic boy being whipped by his parents for going to (Protestant) Sunday school (see below, pp. 129–30), is mentioned in *Old South Meeting,* pp. 156–57. Moody's story is greatly elaborated, ending with the boy's death, while the comparable incident cited in the other source has him end by becoming a Sunday-school teacher. Probably, however, the stock of such characters and stories was common. Such a conclusion is suggested also by similar uses of Bible passages by revivalists. We find Moody using the Old Testament story of the brazen serpent to make the point, "just look to Christ"; it was used in exactly the same way in sermons by the Methodist evangelist Mrs. Maggie Van Cott (see her *The Harvest and the Reaper: Reminiscences of Revival Work* [New York: N. Tibbals & Sons, 1876], p. 324); and by Absalom B. Earle in his most famous sermon (*Bringing in Sheaves* [Boston: James H. Earle, 1868], pp. 128–44). We seem to have here a popular anecdotal-exegetical tradition which deserves fuller investigation.

22. For a listing and samples of objects of prayer, see *Old South Meeting,* pp. 112–18.

23. Prime has a whole chapter devoted to such accounts; see *Fifteen*

Years, pp. 232–52; cf. pp. 36–38. Thompson in *Times,* pp. 307–10, discusses the mother's influence on a man's childhood, with benefits to be reaped later.

24. Fish, *Handbook,* p. 134.

25. A notable exception is Henry Ward Beecher, who rose to prominence slightly earlier than Moody. For a sample of preaching styles, see the sermons in *The New York Pulpit in the Revival of 1858, a Memorial Volume of Sermons* (New York: Sheldon, Blakeman & Co., 1858). From the compilation by Walter P. Doe, *Eminent Authors on Effective Revival Preaching* (Providence, R.I.: A. Greene, 1876), it is evident that the older "expository" approach was not yet dead in revivalism even in Moody's time, while "topical" preaching, the Moody style, was becoming acceptable to some. For illuminating comments on a range of 1870 preachers, see Daniel Calhoun, *The Intelligence of a People* (Princeton, N.J.: Princeton University Press, 1973), pp. 256–90.

26. I have found very few examples of lay exhortations, but see the verbatim report of a prayer meeting in *Old South Meeting,* pp. 65–92, for brief illustrations. If those are representative, the exhortation often included testimony and ran on into prayer.

The Goodspeed and Hall/Stuart accounts are full of comments on Moody's style; see also Findlay's description in *Dwight L. Moody,* pp. 219–26. Moody was so famous for his anecdotes that an enterprising associate, J. B. McClure, collected them, mostly from newspaper accounts, and sold them as *Anecdotes and Illustrations of D. L. Moody* (Chicago: Rhodes & McClure, 1878). Finney had advocated the use of "everyday" illustrations, but his published sermons still employ the carefully arranged and numbered forms of argument. One finds the same adherence to the old pattern in even later and more anecdotal addresses by the evangelist A. B. Earle, while Maggie Van Cott, his contemporary, had abandoned the strict logical form. She still remained with the tradition, however, in that she stuck closely to one scriptural text.

Another question of interest is that or oral versus written style, raised especially by Bruce A. Rosenberg in *The Art of the American Folk Preacher* (New Haven: Yale University Press, 1970). As my analysis is not centered on sermons, I will make only a very few suggestions here, but it does appear that Moody may have been in the tradition of folk preaching. He preached only from very brief notes, which served as little more than cues to Scripture references or anecdotes he already knew well (see McLoughlin, *Modern Revivalism,* p. 244). He sometimes took on the highly excited style of a folk preacher: one of Goodspeed's informants reported that "many times he suffers under very strong emotions, and his thoughts come so fast, and sometimes in such confused forms, that he is wholly unable to find relief in words" (*Wonderful Career,* p. 468), and other accounts mention the rapid tempo of his preaching. More importantly, it is clear that he used basic story structures, elaborating them differently on different occasions with greater or less effectiveness, sometimes forgetting segments and recovering them later. Moody's style seems, insofar as we can judge from transcripts, to have been rhythmically repetitive at times, and formulaic; many passages can be written in the oral-poetry scheme used by Rosenberg (for example, the closing passages of his sermon, "Regeneration," in *Glad Tidings,* pp. 95–96). If this is the case, it raises the question of where Moody learned the style, how widespread it was in the Northeast, and what is the relation of the "folk preaching" tradition to urban revivalism in general. That folk preaching was known in the North, or at least in the Midwest, is shown by a comment in praise of Maggie Van Cott, that she did *not* sound like such a preacher: "Supplemental syllables, such as 'Gospel-ah,' grave-ah and so on, with every terminal word, she is quite clear from such failings, and withal grandly earnest in her work" (quoted from a Wisconsin newspaper in Van Cott, *Harvest,* p. 350). These sorts of questions would appear to be a field for fruitful study, if source materials from different regions and periods are available.

27. In this country the method came to be associated with the name of Moody himself as a particular "school" of interpretation; see Ernest R. Sandeen, *The Roots of Fundamentalism* (Chicago: University of Chicago Press, 1970), pp. 136–39; J. C. Pollock, *Moody: A Biographical Portrait of the Pacesetter in Modern Mass Evangelism* (New York: Macmillan Co., 1963), pp. 72–74.

28. Moody, *Anecdotes,* pp. 27–28.

29. Ibid., pp. 49–50.

30. Moody, "Faith," in *Glad Tidings,* pp. 178–79; and "Compassion of Christ," ibid., p. 201.

31. Moody, *Anecdotes,* p. 43.

32. Moody, *Glad Tidings,* pp. 354–55. For comments on the effectiveness of the domestic appeal, see Goodspeed, *Wonderful Career,* pp. 306, 412.

33. Moody's sermons seldom touched on an analysis of "feeling" as such; indeed, he seemed to think that people worried too much about their feelings and not enough about the matter of deciding for Christ. In his sermon on "Excuses" he discussed the problem: " ' I can't feel.'

That's the last excuse. . . . With some people it is feel, feel, feel all the time. . . . Suppose a gentleman asked me to dinner. I say, 'I will see how I feel.' 'Sick?' he might ask. 'No; it depends on how I feel.' That is not the question—it is whether I will accept the invitation or not. The question with us is, Will we accept salvation—will you believe? There is not a word about feelings in the Scriptures." (The quotation is from Moody, *Great Joy,* pp. 129–30; cf. Moody, *Anecdotes,* pp. 186–87, and the discussion quoted in Hall and Stuart, *Evangelists,* p. 349, for similar statements.) Richard Anderson makes a similar point in his "The Urban Revivalists, 1880–1910" (Ph.D. diss., University of Chicago, 1974), p. 215: "The sermons were indeed sentimental, but the call to converts at the conclusion was directed to the mind and will."

At one level, Moody's comments are contrary to fact: his sermons, and the revivals as a whole, did arouse strong emotions in audiences. Yet from another perspective, his statements are congruent with my assessment of the domestic images in Chapter 4: they were not merely good to feel but good to think. Moody wanted his listeners to accept his portrait of the world, to find it convincing, to decide that "this is how things stand." In a world of turmoil such as he described, the clear-thinking person (so he believed) could do only one thing, namely turn to Jesus as refuge.

34. Moody, *Anecdotes,* pp. 66–67.

35. Ibid., pp. 40–41.

36. Besides disasters, Moody also adds a feature which may be idiosyncratic to him, namely details of maiming and multilation, especially in characters who are to be saved or who save others. In one story, for example, he tells of a man trying to swim to a lifeboat and climb in; but the other occupants prevent him by slicing off his hand. He tries again, but they cut off his other hand. Finally he grabs the edge of the boat with his teeth and, not wanting to cut off his head, they allow him in (see "Seek the Lord While He May Be Found," in *Glad Tidings,* p. 141). In the context of his sermons, the parallel for such mutilations and other deformities is, in Moody's phrase, "the mangled body of the Son of God." I have not found such images to be prominent in contemporaneous sermons by other preachers, nor are they very prominent in the gospel hymns—although a few very popular ones, like "There Is a Fountain" and "There's Power in the Blood," emphasize the bloody death of Jesus. Other preachers do use the general disaster stories, however, and these were probably common stock of the tradition, a more graphic development of the long-standing revival convention of calling attention to the threat of death or the saintly death of a loved

one. See, for example, the storm-at-sea illustrations of Van Cott, *Harvest,* pp. 314–15, and the war story of Earle, in *Sheaves,* pp. 140–41.

37. Moody, *Glad Tidings,* pp. 32–42. An excellent example, though unfortunately too long to quote here, of Moody's fleshing out of biblical characters is his version of the story of the blind man Bartimeus, from Luke 18:35–38 (and Mark 10:32–34). It appears in the sermon, "Christ's Mission to the World," in *Glad Tidings,* pp. 118–19.

38. Moody, *Anecdotes,* p. 14.

39. Some older hymns were kept and used, of course, like Wesley's, although they were often sung to new tunes. Fish saw the preservation of old hymns as part of God's plan and even justified the use of Roman Catholic hymns in this vein: "Though they [the hymns] sometimes disappeared, they never sank; but as engineers for destruction send bombs that, rising high up in wide curves, overleap great spaces and drop down in a distant spot, so God, in times of darkness, seems to have caught up these hymns, spanning long periods of time, and letting them fall at distant eras, not for explosion and wounding, but for healing and consolation" (*Handbook,* p. 307).

40. Thompson, *Times,* p. 350. The parallelism was not only recognized by observers, but was also explicit in Moody's and Sankey's understandings of their meetings. See Goodspeed, *Wonderful Career,* pp. 385, 583, and Hall and Stuart, *Evangelists,* pp. 20, 252, 398.

41. Goodspeed, *Wonderful Career,* p. 71.

42. See, for example, the analysis of the "qualities" of the different keys (citing the authority of a recent biography of Haydn and Mozart) in the review of Hastings and Mason's hymnal, in the *Quarterly Christian Spectator,* 3rd ser., 6 (1834): 217–18.

43. Thompson, *Times,* p. 319.

44. Fish, *Handbook,* p. 302.

45. Thompson, *Times,* p. 353.

46. Fish, *Handbook,* p. 324.

47. Hall and Stuart, *Evangelists,* pp. 208–9.

48. Ira D. Sankey, *Sankey's Story of the Gospel Hymns and of Sacred Songs and Solos* (Philadelphia: Sunday School Times Co., 1906), pp. 232–33.

Chapter 6
Social Religion and Passionate Politics: The Situation of the Hymns

1. For the tradition which connects evangelical affiliation, nativist tendencies, and reform to the emergence of the Republican party, see

Ronald P. Formisano, *The Birth of Mass Political Parties: Michigan, 1827–1861* (Princeton: Princeton University Press, 1971). For the identification of the evangelical churches with sound money and Republicanism after the Civil War, see Henry F. May, *Protestant Churches and Industrial America* (New York: Harper and Row, 1967), pp. 43–44. Most leading Northern denominational papers leaned Republican in the 1870s, though many opposed Grant. And the affiliation of churches with parties did not go unnoticed within the denominations themselves; for example, the Methodist *Northwestern Christian Advocate* observed in 1875 that denominations had often been identified with particular parties and, most recently, the Methodists with the Republicans (Sept. 15, 1875, p. 4).

2. William G. McLoughlin, Jr., *Modern Revivalism: Charles Grandison Finney to Billy Graham* (New York: Ronald Press, 1959), pp. 168, 257; Bernard A. Weisberger, *They Gathered at the River* (Chicago: Quadrangle Books, 1958), p. 169. The term "intellectually unsophisticated" is somewhat misleading; certainly Moody's audiences would have been literate and regular consumers of popular literature, but not theologically sophisticated.

3. Since Weisberger's account is of the great revivalists, he deals only ephemerally with the 1857–58 revival; McLoughlin describes it, but only as a response to economic conditions.

4. Weisberger, *River,* pp. 163, 169; McLoughlin, *Modern Revivalism,* p. 168. An account richer in specifics but with essentially the same viewpoint appears in James F. Findlay, Jr., *Dwight L. Moody: American Evangelist, 1837–1899* (Chicago: University of Chicago Press, 1969), pp. 285–302.

5. McLoughlin, *Modern Revivalism,* p. 7.

6. Ibid., p. 169; similar points are made and ignored by Findlay, *Dwight L. Moody,* pp. 290, 297.

7. I base those statements on extensive reading in the popular religious press, not theological journals. Henry Ward Beecher's *Christian Union* was the largest in circulation for the early 1870s—as large as the biggest secular weeklies—but dropped off sharply after his trial began in 1874. For a supplement from the Congregational-Presbyterian heritage, I have used the *Independent* (New York), which was by then virtually nondenominational like Beecher's paper. It was smaller in circulation but an extremely influential religious weekly. To represent the Methodist tradition, as the largest Northern body, without a theocratic heritage, and the Western section of the North, I have chosen the *Northwestern Christian Advocate* (Chicago). To have a crosscheck on

issues from the secular press, I used *Harper's Weekly,* one of the largest miscellanies published. It had in this period a strong evangelical and Republican bias, but rarely dealt with religious issues specifically. For information on these and other journals, see Frank Luther Mott, *A History of American Magazines* (5 vols. (Cambridge: Harvard University Press, 1938–57), vol. 3: *1865–1885*; and Mott, *American Journalism: A History, 1690–1960* (3rd ed.; New York: Macmillan Company, 1962). I have used the *Independent* as the main source for the 1857–58 commentaries, with less systematic examination of secular papers like the *New York Tribune* and *New York Times* and random checks of other papers in both periods like the *Congregationalist* and Boston's *Zion's Herald.* The papers show, in the early 1870s, generally positive attitudes toward the achievements of science and biblical research and a dubious but condescending attitude toward evolution. The defensive hysterics of later years are nowhere in evidence. Specifically religious issues tended to be intrachurch, for example, a fight over the formulation of the creed in Presbyterianism, arguments over the presiding eldership in Methodism.

8. McLoughlin, *Modern Revivalism,* pp. 6–7.

9. Part of the problem here is McLoughlin's concept of an awakening as extending over an "age." There were, in his scheme, four awakenings: 1725–50, 1795–1835, 1875–1915, and 1945–?. If any of those rather lengthy periods *had* corresponded to an economic or political crisis, it is doubtful the nation would have survived. The scheme requires also that he dismiss the 1857–58 revival as an accident, related to an economic depression—a grave error, in my judgment. It is noteworthy too that the earlier revivals of Nettleton-Beecher, then of Finney, were in politically turbulent periods, the first during the decline of Federalism, the second concurrent with the rise of Jacksonianism and the beginnings of the second-party system. Historians of the benevolent societies have argued for strong political connections in the first case. Formisano in *Mass Political Parties* has suggested important parallels and common traditions in the second.

10. For these developments and especially the ideology of the "Slave Power," see Eric Foner, *Free Soil, Free Labor, Free Men: The Ideology of the Republican Party before the Civil War* (New York: Oxford University Press, 1970), and Formisano, *Mass Political Parties,* Ch. 12. We now know too, as McLoughlin and Weisberger did not, that evangelicals were deeply involved in politics, and increasingly so in the early 1850s. Formisano summarizes his conclusions about the relation of evangelicalism to the emergence of the Republican party as follows: "Thus in

the 1850s a political evangelicalism became revived, politicized, and broadened by anti-Popery, nativism, temperance zeal, and other Protestant moralisms. Then it married itself, through anti-Southernism, to an egalitarian tradition with which it had earlier been a natural political enemy. Earlier, the secularism of egalitarianism had created incompatibility between the two. The Pope and the slaveholder gave them common ground on which to fuse" (p. 330).

11. McLoughlin, *Modern Revivalism,* p. 163.

12. See William R. Taylor, *Cavalier and Yankee* (New York: Harper & Row, 1961), for the opposing ideologies. Foner has criticized Taylor for holding that concern over Yankee character was prevalent "everywhere," but does not doubt that it was an element in the Northern self-understanding (*Free Soil,* p. 54).

13. *Independent,* March 4, 1858, p. 4.

14. See especially S. Irenaeus Prime, *Fifteen Years of Prayer in the Fulton Street Meeting* (New York: Scribner, Armstrong, & Co., 1872), pp. 48–49, 136, 139, 273–89, 290–309. "It would almost seem," he writes, "that we are fast becoming a nation of drunkards" (p. 299); and he refers to the "enormity of the sin of intemperance and the flood of ruin which is sweeping over the land" (p. 309). The sin of drink often follows, he implies, failure in business, and then—in the standard domino theory—leads to thoughts of suicide (pp. 308–9), that is, to insanity.

15. Editorial, *Northwestern Christian Advocate,* Aug. 11, 1875, p. 4; cf. the article by N. A. Patterson, ibid., Feb. 23, 1876, p. 1; and the editorial, *Christian Union,* Aug. 26, 1874, p. 16.

16. See Foner, *Free Soil,* for comments on this in the earlier part of the century; and Keith Ian Polakoff, *The Politics of Inertia* (Baton Rouge: Louisiana State University Press, 1973), ch. 1, for the organization of politics in the 1870s.

17. The term and its use in this type of context is from Jonathan Z. Smith, "A Pearl of Great Price and a Cargo of Yams," *History of Religions* 16 (1976): 1–19.

18. On the political background, see Polakoff, *Politics*; on Beecher, see Paul Carter, *The Spiritual Crisis of the Gilded Age* (De Kalb, Ill: Northern Illinois University Press, 1971), pp. 109–32; on the Whiskey Ring, Gen. John McDonald, *Secrets of the Great Whiskey Ring* (1880; rpt., New York: Burt Franklin, 1969). The latter was especially damaging; for, as the *Northwestern Christian Advocate* observed, it was bad enough to make and sell whiskey, but now a legal crime had been added to the moral offense (editorial, Dec. 8, 1875, p. 4). For Lowell's poem, "Agassiz," see *Christian Union,* July 15, 1874, p. 38.

19. For the decisions, see John F. Wilson, ed., *Church and State in American History* (Boston: D. C. Heath, 1965), pp. 121–26.

20. This summary follows John Higham, *Strangers in the Land* (New Brunswick, N.J.: Rutgers University Press, 1955), pp. 28–29.

21. *Independent,* Sept. 9, 1875, p. 16; cf. editorial, Sept. 23, 1875, p. 17; and the article by Thomas Wentworth Higginson, Sept. 30, 1875, p. 1, admitting that "the prediction is constantly made that we are on the verge of 'a religious conflict which threatens the very existence of our Republic,' " but disparaging such pessimism.

22. *Harper's Weekly,* May 8, 1875, p. 384. The accompanying article said that the Republicans had a "close identification . . . with the cause of education" because of their connection with the program of education for freedmen in the South. Democrats and Catholics were therefore against education; in fact Catholic education was none at all (p. 385).

23. Editorial, *Northwestern Christian Advocate,* Aug. 11, 1875, p. 4.

24. *Independent,* Sept. 16, 1875, p. 1. The connection between voting and praying was not new. Formisano, in *Mass Political Parties,* quotes a Methodist minister's sermon in the early 1850s (which Formisano describes as "not easily distinguishable from a campaign speech") as saying that " 'conscience extends to the ballot box. . . . It is just as much a moral act to vote as to pray. Indeed, every vote which we deposit is the invocation of a curse or a blessing upon the land' " (pp. 249–50). See also the *Independent* editorial for Oct. 7, 1875, p. 16: "Negative preparation for a vast advance in the religious world has been made during the past two years. Trust in money and in man has been signally weakened. . . . Mistrust and suspicion are disintegrating political parties and paralyzing trade and commerce. Thus, by being emptied and swept of other trust, men's hearts are being prepared for that which is pure and safe and permanent."

25. *Northwestern Christian Advocate,* Sept. 22, 1875, p. 4. The clamor for "the revival we need" was apparently widespread. The *Northwestern* in another editorial on Jan. 5, 1876, p. 4, cited the Cuyler article, Boston's *Zion's Herald,* the New York *Christian Advocate,* and the *Congregationalist* as all pleading for the same thoroughgoing reformation of morals.

26. Rufus Clark, *The Work of God in Great Britain: Under Messrs. Moody and Sankey, 1873 to 1875* (New York: Harper & Brothers, 1875), p. 371. It should be noted here that British accolades were an important factor in the evangelists' American reception, as McLoughlin has also observed (*Modern Revivalism,* p. 199). Unlike the 1857–58 case,

this revival may have needed the two stars to get off the ground. The press portrayed them as plain men who attracted the majority of British Protestants and to whom eventually even the upper classes had to listen—a victory for people's religion, so to speak, over the "dead forms" of high churchmen and nobles (see John V. Farwell's essay, *Independent,* Aug. 5, 1875, p. 3; and the accounts of the evangelists' visit to Eton College which created a stir in the House of Lords, in *Independent,* July 8, 1875, p. 4, and *New York Times,* June 22, 1875, sec. 6, p. 1; also Findlay, *Dwight L. Moody,* p. 179). Not all American readers may have known that England had just undergone a reformation of worship, but the comparison with Catholicism was clear in phrases like "dead forms." A discussion of the reforms did appear in the *Northwestern,* Aug. 4, 1875, p. 4.

Appendix: Methods of Analyzing the Hymns

1. Fernandez, "Persuasions and Performances," in *Myth, Symbol, and Culture,* ed. Clifford Geertz (New York: W. W. Norton & Co., 1971), see especially pp. 41–48.

2. That assumption is based on ideas taken from recent semantic theory, namely: (1) that a word acquires part of its sense from its place in a system of relationships to other words in the vocabulary; (2) that certain sets of words are related to each other "paradigmatically," that is, are mutually substitutable but incompatible in the same syntactic location; and (3) that the choice of one word over another constitutes part of its meaning. For discussion of the relevant concepts, see John Lyons, *Introduction to Theoretical Linguistics* (Cambridge: Cambridge University Press, 1968), pp. 412–14, 427–29, 453–60.

3. Dickson Bruce, *And They All Sang Hallelujah: Plain-Folk Camp-Meeting Religion, 1800–1845* (Knoxville: University of Tennessee Press, 1974); see especially pp. 84–86.

4. James C. Downey, "The Gospel Hymn, 1875–1930" (M. Mus. thesis, University of Southern Mississippi, 1963), p. 118; for musical elements of the chorus, p. 142.

5. For discussion of the basic methods and some of the pros and cons, see Bernard Berelson, *Content Analysis in Communications Research* (Glencoe, Ill.: Free Press, 1952), especially ch. 3—this work is the classic; Alexander L. George, "Quantitative and Qualitative Approaches to Content Analysis," in *Trends in Content Analysis,* ed. I. de Sola Pool (Urbana, Ill.: University of Illinois Press, 1959), pp. 7–39;

George Gerbner, "On Content Analysis and Critical Research in Mass Communication," in *People, Society, and Mass Communications,* ed. Lewis Anthony Dexter and David Manning White (New York: Free Press, 1964), pp. 476–500; and Ole R. Holsti, *Content Analysis for the Social Sciences and Humanities* (Reading, Mass.: Addison-Wesley, 1969), esp. pp. 1–23. For an interpretation of the state of the field, see Berelson, "The State of Communication Research" in the Dexter and White volume. Examples of application are numerous; for the use of the method with different kinds of materials, see Berelson and Patricia J. Salter, "Majority and Minority Americans: An Analysis of Magazine Fiction," *Public Opinion Quarterly* 10 (1946): 168–90; Robert S. Frank, *Message Dimensions of Television News* (Lexington, Mass.: D. C. Heath, 1973); and Benjamin N. Colby, "Cultural Patterns in Narrative," *Science* 151 (1966): 793–98, the latter being an application to traditional folklore materials and relatively less successful, I think, because Colby's materials seem to be heterogeneous.

6. Kenneth Burke, *Philosophy of Literary Form* (Baton Rouge: Louisiana State University Press, 1941), pp. 20–25.

Index

Index to Names and Subjects

Index to Hymns Cited
(by first line and by common title)